misplaced myths & lost legends

misplaced myths & lost legends

adam bushnell

A SAGE company
2455 Teller Road
Thousand Oaks, California 91320
(0800)233-9936
www.corwin.com

SAGE Publications Ltd
1 Oliver's Yard
55 City Road
London EC1Y 1SP

SAGE Publications India Pvt Ltd
B 1/I 1 Mohan Cooperative Industrial Area
Mathura Road
New Delhi 110 044

SAGE Publications Asia-Pacific Pte Ltd
3 Church Street
#10-04 Samsung Hub
Singapore 049483

Editor: Amy Thornton
Senior project editor: Chris Marke
Cover design: Wendy Scott
Typeset by: C&M Digitals (P) Ltd, Chennai, India
Printed in the UK

Library of Congress Control Number: 2022933186

British Library Cataloguing in Publication Data

A catalogue record for this book is available from the British Library.

ISBN 978-1-5297-9155-6
ISBN 978-1-5297-9154-9 (pbk)

At SAGE we take sustainability seriously. Most of our products are printed in the UK using responsibly sourced papers and boards. When we print overseas we ensure sustainable papers are used as measured by the PREPS grading system. We undertake an annual audit to monitor our sustainability.

Contents

About the author

Adam Bushnell is a full-time author who delivers creative writing workshops in the UK and internationally in both state and private education to all ages.

His books have been selected by the School Library Association for the *Boys into Books* recommended reading list. Previously a teacher, Adam now also delivers continuing personal development (CPD) to teachers and others working in education on how to inspire writing in the classroom.

Introduction

After reading a collection of Ancient Greek myths as a child, I decided that I wanted to become an author. The heroes, monsters, gods and goddesses absolutely captivated my imagination, and they still do to this day. Myths, legends, folk and fairy tales have been the basis and inspiration for all of my writing, but my most favourite thing to do is to use them to inspire children to write in the classroom.

The stories in this book are all traditional tales. There are myths (meaning completely made up), legends (meaning they have some elements of truth, such as characters that actually existed) and folk tales (stories that have been passed down orally). I have written them exactly as I have told them to children. They are written to be read aloud to a class. I recommend that you read each story first before choosing which ones to use with your children, as some are more suited to upper KS2 than to KS1. There are stories of ghosts, demons and monsters which are intended for older children.

The stories have been collected from across the United Kingdom. There are twenty stories in total, with five from Wales, five from Northern Ireland, five from Scotland and five from England. However, there are variations in many of these stories from each county in the United Kingdom, as well as across Europe and beyond. I have referenced this in the introduction to each story. The short history behind the origin of the story can also be shared with children.

Once you have read a story to your class, each tale then has creative writing activities for the children. These can be adapted very easily according to the year group that you teach. There are narrative story-writing opportunities, character and setting descriptions, action scenes, dialogue and more. The following table lists each chapter with a description of the contents.

Chapter	Description
1. The fish of wisdom (Irish)	Introducing the character Finn McCool and looking at the story of how he became wise.
	Activities follow based around the creation of a character with a super power. Then hyperbole boasting follows.
2. The Sockburn worm (English)	The story is about a legless dragon that can breathe poisonous gases.
	The children design their own worm and describe its powers. There is also a Jabberwocky-style poem.
3. Monday, Tuesday (Irish)	A fairy tale of kindness and looking after the environment.
	Activities follow describing the setting of Fairyland, plus letter writing.
4. The witch cats (Welsh)	A story about witches who can turn into cats.
	The children use show-and-not-tell writing techniques to describe a witch turning into different animals and the reader has to guess the animal.
5. Jack and the beanstalk (English)	The first story of the character Jack. Other Jack stories follow in later chapters.
	Pupils retell the story-making changes to the characters, objects and settings.
6. The rich lord's wife (Welsh)	A story about a girl who uses her intelligence to outwit a rich suitor.
	Activities follow to describe the two opposite characters in detail using figurative language.
7. The unicorn (Scottish)	A story about the healing powers of the mythical creature.
	The children design and describe their own mythical creature, including verbs and adverbs.
8. Tattercoats (English)	A Cinderella-like story.
	Pupils design and describe their own 'nature clothing' worn by a Green Man and a Green Woman.
9. The leprechaun (Irish)	A story of the trickster and his gold.
	The children write riddles in the style of the leprechaun and imagine the treasure they get for solving them.
10. Whuppity Stoorie (Scottish)	A Rumpelstiltskin-style story in which the main character has to guess the name of the witch.
	Pupils write potions with nonsense language and describe the magic that happens.
11. The cow that ate the piper (Scottish)	A ghost story with a twist in the tale.
	The children plan their own ghost story using some elements from the tale: a ghost character, setting, reason why and a cliffhanger ending.

Chapter	Description
12. Jack the Giant Killer (English)	The further adventures of Jack. He meets a variety of giants and kills them all.
	Pupils design more giants for Jack to battle, then create nonsense alliteration and describe the action scenes of how he does it.
13. The Draiglin Hogney (Scottish)	A tale of a demon who traps people to make them his slaves.
	The children describe a demon character with magic weapons and armour.
14. The white dragon and the red dragon (Welsh)	A metaphorical story that describes how the Romans were chased from Wales.
	Activities follow on metaphorical descriptions of characters.
15. Jack and the fish (English)	Jack meets the devil and tricks him with the help of a fishy friend.
	The children solve trickster puzzles in the style of the story.
16. Abhartach the vampire (Irish)	The story of an evil, dwarf-like creature that can turn itself into any animal or even become invisible.
	Character descriptions include hair, eyes, nose, skin, teeth, chin, clothes, hands, fingers, nails, etc.
17. Tammy and the trows (Scottish)	A boy escapes from a family of trolls.
	The children write an action scene using a storyboard.
18. The king's secret (Welsh)	The king has horse's ears, but it is a secret he wishes no one to know.
	Activities follow on retelling techniques focusing on dialogue. The children write a playscript based on the story.
19. Jack-o'-lantern (Irish)	A final Jack story on why we have pumpkins at Hallowe'en.
	The children write descriptions of spooky characters. They use antonyms and synonyms.
20. Sir Gawain and the Green Knight (Welsh)	The Knight of the Round Table faces an immortal foe, but Sir Gawain's honesty and valour win through.
	Pupils write a character description with heraldry, then plan a short myth.

As an author and a teacher, I think that myths and legends are critical in schools and at home. The more we share them, the more they can help children and adults to understand the way of the world. The stories contain adventure, action, tragedy, comedy and, most importantly, hope. They can inspire children, as they did me as a child, to become writers. It is my hope that this book will be useful to you and help with creative writing opportunities in your classroom.

Adam Bushnell

1 The fish of wisdom (Irish)

Fionn mac Cumhaill, known in English as Finn McCool, is a giant hero from Irish folklore. Fionn's son Oisín narrates the great deeds of Fionn in poetry. Perhaps the most famous story of Fionn is that of the Giant's Causeway, which tells of Fionn's battle with the Scottish giant Benandonner. In the story, Fionn lifted great rocks from the Antrim coastline and hurled them into the sea to make a path to reach Benandonner after the giant threatened Ireland. When Fionn crossed the path he had laid and he saw the size of Benandonner, he retreated to Ireland where his wife disguised him as a baby. When Benandonner crossed the path to find Fionn, the giant saw the baby and realised that the father of the baby must be huge. Benandonner ran back to Scotland and threw most of the path into the sea so that he couldn't be followed. The remains of the path is what the Giant's Causeway looks like today. In the story that we have here, Fionn wishes to be as wise as his wife who tricked Benandonner. So Fionn travels to see the poet and teacher Finegas to learn how to be wise.

The fish of wisdom

Fionn mac Cumhaill travelled all along the River Boyne searching for the wise druid named Finegas. The serpentine river coiled its way across Ireland and Fionn followed. Eventually, he found himself at a hut beside a well. A man dressed in white robes and wearing a wreath of green leaves stepped out of the hut as Fionn approached. The man's white beard was dense and long, but Fionn could still see the warm smile beneath it.

'Greetings,' said the man. 'My name is Finegas.'

'At last!' beamed Fionn. 'I've been searching for you for days.'

'I know,' smiled Finegas.

'How?' asked Fionn.

'I listen.'

'To what?'

'The birds, the trees and the wind.'

'Can you teach me?' asked Fionn with wide eyes.

'Only those who can listen can learn.'

Fionn nodded eagerly.

'Then let us begin,' Finegas said with another smile.

The two of them went into the hut and Fionn's lessons started straight away. He learnt of nature and weather, heard stories from long ago that had meaning and how to pass this knowledge on to others through oral stories. In the evening, Finegas taught Fionn about the stars and planets. He was taught how to use the night sky to navigate this land and other worlds beyond.

After a few weeks Finegas sat Fionn down and told him about a very special fish.

'It's the salmon of knowledge,' explained Finegas. 'It lives there in the Tobar Seghais.'

'That well?' asked Fionn.

Finegas nodded. 'It leapt from the river and into the well. There it came to know all things of the universe.'

'How?'

'You see that tree?' asked Finegas.

He pointed towards a gigantic hazel tree. Its branches were covered in thick emerald green leaves and the trunk was made up of lots of other trunks. Fionn felt dizzy trying to count them all.

'The first thing that was ever made was that tree. The world grew around it. That's why my hut is right here, so that I can learn from the tree.'

Fionn walked over to the tree and stroked the smooth bark. Finegas followed and continued.

'The salmon now lives in this well.'

There was a large stone well beneath the tree. Fionn had been carrying buckets of fresh water from the well to the hut every morning for weeks and paid it little attention. He peered down into the dark water now looking for movement beneath the still water.

'Hazel nuts fall from the tree into the well. The salmon ate the nuts and became the keeper of all the world's knowledge.'

'Can't you just eat the hazel nuts then?' asked Fionn.

Fingegas shook his head with a little laugh.

'No, the fish holds the knowledge now. The tree has passed it on to the fish and the fish will pass it on to a human.'

'Who?' Fionn gasped with wide eyes. 'It's you, isn't it?'

'I've been trying to catch that fish for many, many years now, but I just can't do it.'

'Can I try?'

Fionn stared at the old druid while the moments passed.

'Of course you can,' smiled Finegas.

Fionn raced off to the hut delightedly. He grabbed a rod and some bait and bolted back to the well.

'Good luck!' called Finegas and left Fionn to it.

Fionn spent all that day and the next trying to catch the fish, but there wasn't even a ripple.

'Are you sure the salmon is in there?' Fionn said at last, exasperated. 'How do you know it hasn't jumped back into the river?'

'He's in there all right, but he's more cunning than you and me combined.'

After a week had passed, Fionn gave up.

'It's no use. I'll never catch it.'

'Perhaps I will have one last try,' Finegas said, taking the rod.

He dropped the baited hook into the well of Tobar Segias, then sat and waited. Hours turned into days and still Finegas sat by the well. Fionn offered to take over from his teacher, but Finegas shook his head. He didn't eat or drink. He didn't sleep.

Three days had now passed when Fionn was woken by a mighty cheer and shriek.

'I've caught it!' bellowed Finegas. 'I have the salmon of knowledge!'

Fionn leapt from his bed and ran to the well. Finegas was standing next to it with a sparkling salmon held in both hands. The fish was huge with rainbow-coloured scales and bright, silver eyes.

'What happens now?' asked Fionn.

'Now I shall eat it!' beamed Finegas.

'Let me cook it for you. You need to rest.'

As if suddenly remembering how exhausted he felt, Finegas nodded. He felt the knots in his shoulders, the bags under his eyes and the heavy weight of the fish all at once. He handed the salmon over to Fionn and trudged back to the hut to wash and change.

Fionn carefully placed the salmon on to a soft fur rug and began to prepare a fire. He collected the bark from a silver birch tree and snapped some thin dry sticks. After collecting some larger dry sticks, he began to build a small tent shape around the birch bark. He used some flint to get some sparks that ignited the bark. Soon the smaller sticks were alight and he added the larger ones.

Then Fionn cut open the fish with his knife. He cleaned out the guts and washed his hands in the river. After skewering the salmon on a large clean stick, he began to roast it. He slowly turned it this way and that over the flames. Soon the fish began to smell delicious and the skin began to go crispy.

'Ow!' he suddenly cried out.

He had burned his thumb on the hot fish skin. The thumb glowed and was angry red, and Fionn sucked it to ease the pain. Some of the juices from the fish filled his mouth with flavour. It was zesty and delicious. Fionn suddenly felt something else, though. He felt himself becoming wise. He began to understand the language of the birds and the ways of this world. He knew the tides and understood time.

A sudden rush of guilt filled him entirely. The fish was for Finegas. He took the fish to the hut. Perhaps only a little of the knowledge had been passed to Fionn. Yet he knew this was not the case, for he knew everything.

'Ah, there you are!' Finegas beamed as Fionn entered the hut carrying the fish.

Fionn couldn't look his teacher in the eye. He offered the fish while staring at the floor.

'Whatever is wrong?' asked Finegas. 'You look as though you've seen a ghost! This is a happy day, you should be . . . oh.'

The teacher understood at once what had happened.

'You tasted the fish.'

'I'm sorry!' Fionn blurted out – his words were rushed and garbled. 'The knowledge was meant for you, not me! I didn't mean to. I burned my thumb on the hot skin while I was cooking it and . . .'

'Stop,' interrupted Finegas. 'It's all right. Don't worry.'

'But *you* were meant to have the knowledge, not me.'

'If that were the case, then I would have it. The knowledge is passed on to who it is *meant* to be passed on to. *You* have this knowledge because *you* will need it, not me.'

'Eat the rest of the fish.'

Fionn sat down and did as instructed. He ate the fish. He knew how to design and construct. He understood the workings of the human body. He knew that the best way to learn was to listen to others, listen to your own inner voice and not to react until all things were considered. He had wisdom.

'There is nothing more for me to teach you,' said Finegas once the fish was finished.

The knowledge that Fionn had gained was to be needed. He went on to become the leader of the Fianna, an army of the greatest warriors the world had ever seen. Whenever Fionn mac Cumhaill needed to call on his new power, all he had to do was to put his thumb in his mouth, which he did many times on his countless adventures.

About this story

Wisdom might well be the greatest gift any of us could have. To understand everything of this world is a super power. Fionn mac Cumhaill used this super power to defeat his enemies, collect treasure, find magical weapons, hunt for wild animals and achieve many other deeds. In legend, it is said that Fionn is not dead but rather sleeping in a cave with his warriors. He will awake when the Fianna hunting horn is sounded three times and then he will defend Ireland from its greatest threat. But, until that time, perhaps new heroes are needed – heroes like the children in your class.

Teaching idea: Choosing a super power

Ask your children to choose their own super power. It could be to do with the brain, such as wisdom, telekinesis, controlling machines with your mind or being able to download new skills whenever you want. Perhaps the super powers could be related to bodies such as strength, agility, speed or camouflage. The children might be able to shoot fog, acid, water or oil from their fingers or blast lasers, lightning, soundwaves or ultraviolet light from their eyes. The website Powerlisting.Fandom.com lists many alternate super powers to explore:

https://powerlisting.fandom.com/wiki/List_of_Supernatural_Powers_and_Abilities

The children could then use their powers like Fionn used his to go on great adventures. Fionn's son, Oisín, retells these events in the form of poetry. Without a poet to call on, the children could retell their own powers in the form of poetry. Therefore, these poems will be in the first person to describe what incredible things they can do.

Before his boxing match in Zaire called 'The Rumble in the Jungle', Mohammad Ali orally described the amazing things he could do, such as.

I've wrestled with alligators,
I've tussled with a whale.
I handcuffed lightning,
And thrown thunder in jail.
Just last week, I murdered a rock,
Injured a stone, hospitalised a brick.
I'm so mean, I make medicine sick.

You could use Ali's 'Rumble in the Jungle' as a template for the children to describe their own great deeds and powers. You could give them the structure of Ali's words, such as:

I handcuffed lightning, I've _____ whale.
I've _____ and thrown thunder in jail.
I _____ a _____, I _____ a brick.
I'm so _____, I make _____ sick.
I'm so fast, I can _____ and don't get wet.
I can run through _____ or _____ and it's no threat.
When _____ meet me, they'll all say _____!
I can _____, and _____ .
I'm like Fionn mac Cumhaill and I'm like Mohammad Ali.
I'm _____ , _____ and _____, that's me!

Older pupils might not need the structure of a template. They might be able to find their own rhyming couplets. However, using this as a model, you might have a poem like:

I handcuffed lightning, I've saved a beached whale.
I've got the power to shoot lightning and thrown thunder in jail.
I befriended a dragon, I made a talking brick.
I'm so incredible, I make Batman and Superman sick.
I'm so fast, I can dive into the sea and don't get wet.
I can run through lava or fire and it's no threat.
When Year Six meet me, they'll all say hoorah!
I can solve any maths problem and then go out to play.
I'm like Fionn mac Cumhaill and I'm like Mohammad Ali.
I'm epic, awesome and fantastic – that's me!

2 The Sockburn worm (English)

In the North of England, a 'burn' is a small river. Many places had 'burn' in the name if they were near a river. Sockburn was a small village near the River Tees. This village is now part of Darlington, but long ago it was a place terrorised by a fearsome dragon. The dragon was known as a 'worm' – not a worm like wiggly woo, but rather a legless dragon. This comes from the Viking word 'wyrm' which means 'dragon'. There are many 'worm' stories from the UK such as 'The Lambton Worm', 'The Bamburgh Worm' and 'The Longwitton Worm'.

The Sockburn worm

Humphrey Conyers was the Lord of Sockburn. He looked out across the rugged hills and meandering river. He decided it was the perfect day for a horse ride. The sun was high and hot, there wasn't a cloud in the sky. He had his mare saddled and readied. Then the horse galloped with thunderous hooves over the land. Humphrey breathed in deeply and couldn't keep the smile from his face.

Just then, though, another sound rumbled over the landscape. It was roaring unlike anything Humphrey had heard before. It consumed the sky and deafened his ears. The horse readied back in fright and Humphrey tumbled to the floor. He landed with a dull thud and the horse raced away terrified.

Humphrey rubbed his sore back and tried to stand up. Then the roar filled everything again. His wild eyes looked this way and that. Suddenly, over the brow of a small hill came a most monstrous sight. With eyes of blazing fire, a dragon slithered towards Humphrey. He cried out in terror and stumbled to his feet. A stench suddenly filled the air. It was a noxious gas of toxic venom that spewed from the dragon's mouth.

Humphrey cried out again as he turned to see biting, snapping jaws spitting green gas as the dragon slid smoothly over the ground. Its serpentine body moved as a snake carving sleek shapes into the soft grass.

The dragon was almost upon Humphrey now burbling its poisonous gas. Humphrey felt dizzy. The toxins began to do their work and he fell to the floor clutching at his throat. Then the dragon opened its jaws and snapped them closed. Humphrey was devoured in one bite.

The dragon had a taste for human flesh now. It terrorised the village daily, gobbling up anyone in its path. People were too terrified to go outside for fear of the dragon's jaws and poison.

Humphrey had a son. His name was John Conyers and he had trained as a page, then a squire and eventually he became a knight. He had been fighting far away but had now returned home. When news of his father's death reached him and he heard about this poisonous dragon, John was distraught. He went straight to All Saints Church in Sockburn village. There, wearing a suit of chainmail armour, he leaned on his sword in front of the altar. He kneeled before God and asked for help to defeat the terrible dragon.

Then, with his coat of mail armour, huge kite shield and falchion sword, he set off to find the dragon. It did not take long. The creature was feasting on a herd of cows in a nearby field. John narrowed his eyes and ran towards the foe. The dragon reared backwards onto its massive tail, opened its wide jaws and spat out a vast stream of toxic gas. John ducked under this and swung his sword. The dragon reared back further, then slammed its body towards the knight. John blocked the creature with his kite shield but was pushed down to his knees. The dragon spat more venomous breath this way and that. John held his breath and began to slash his sword again and again. One, two! One, two! At last the blade stabbed into the dragon, which howled with fury. John pushed it through and through.

The dragon slumped backwards and let out a last breath of green gas. John stepped forward and sliced off the head. Obsidian black blood poured in all directions. John kept the head as a trophy, but kicked part of the dragon's body into the River Tees, then buried the rest beneath the earth. He rolled a large grey stone on top of the grave site to mark the exact place where he had slain the beast.

Holding the head aloft, he marched back to Sockburn to meet a cheering crowd. He threw the head down and took off his helmet. Pulling free his mail coif, he smiled widely. He held out his sword and cried, 'With this falchion I have killed the dragon!'

There was another mighty cheer. News of the victorious knight spread far and wide across the land. The king himself got to hear of John Conyers' great deed. The king gave all the land of Sockburn and the surrounding area to the Conyers family.

Many, many years later, John Conyers died and was buried in a tomb inside Conyers Chapel at All Saints Church in Darlington. You can visit it today and see the stone statue of Sir John Conyers wearing his armour and sleeping peacefully forever more.

About this story

The falchion that was used to killed the Sockburn worm can be seen today in Durham Cathedral. It is now part of the Cathedral's Open Treasure Exhibition. A replica of the sword has also been used for many centuries in ceremonies whenever a new Bishop of Durham is appointed..

Lewis Carroll, author of *Alice in Wonderland*, spent much of his youth near the River Tees. It is said that his poem *The Jabberwocky* was inspired by the stories he heard when he lived in the North of England. Some say that it was the Lambton worm that he used as inspiration and others claim that it was the Sockburn worm. The poem, written in 1872, goes like this:

'Twas brillig, and the slithy toves
Did gyre and gimble in the wabe:
All mimsy were the borogoves,
And the mome raths outgrabe.

'Beware the Jabberwock, my son!
The jaws that bite, the claws that catch!
Beware the Jubjub bird, and shun
The frumious Bandersnatch!'

He took his vorpal sword in hand:
Long time the manxome foe he sought –
So rested he by the Tumtum tree,
And stood awhile in thought.

And, as in uffish thought he stood,
The Jabberwock, with eyes of flame,
Came whiffling through the tulgey wood,
And burbled as it came!

One, two! One, two! And through and through
The vorpal blade went snicker-snack!
He left it dead, and with its head
He went galumphing back.

'And has thou slain the Jabberwock?
Come to my arms, my beamish boy!
O frabjous day! Callooh! Callay!'
He chortled in his joy.

'Twas brillig, and the slithy toves
Did gyre and gimble in the wabe;
All mimsy were the borogoves,
And the mome raths outgrabe.

There are certain similarities between the poem and the story. If authors such as Lewis Carroll can use the story to inspire some writing, then we can certainly do the same in the classroom.

Teaching idea: Designing a worm

The children could begin by designing their own worm, ensuring that their legless dragons have long, snake-like bodies, but also add other features such as multiple heads, wings, claws, spikes, horns, scales, stripes, spots, etc.

Once designed, the children could then label their worms with nouns such as eyes, nostrils, teeth, tongue, etc. Adjectives could then be added to the nouns, including the colour, size, shape, texture, mood, etc. The children will then have gathered noun phrases which could be used in their writing later.

The children could next begin to think about the powers their worms could have. We know that the Sockburn worm could breathe out poisonous gases. But tell the children about other powerful worms such as the Longwitton worm which was invincible as long as its tail was inside its cave. The Lambton worm could join itself back together if it was cut into pieces. The children could add their own powers and you could suggest some such as fire, ice, lava, lasers, lightning, an extendable tongue, etc.

While the powers are being added to their worm design, the children could also begin to gather verbs to accompany these powers such as:

breathing fire;
blasting ice;
spewing lava;
shooting lasers;
firing lightning;
extending tongue.

Other verbs could also be added to do with how it moves, the sounds it makes, how it hunts, etc.

You could ask questions as prompts, such as:

Where does it sleep?
What do the eyes do?
How does it eat?
Where does it go?
Where did it come from?
What does it like to do?
What doesn't it like to do?

To help the children remember the verbs, they could stand up and do the action when you call out the verb. For example:

flying, stomping, charging, gliding, slithering, squeezing, biting, roaring, hunting, sneaking, growling, hissing, etc.

The children could then write down the actions that they can remember. After that, adverbs could also be added to the verbs. You could give some word banks of adverbs that are grouped together according to meaning. For example, if the worm could move at speed, you could then write:

quickly, swiftly, speedily, rapidly, hastily or fast.

It is worthwhile pointing out to the children that adverbs usually end with 'ly', but there are exceptions such as 'fast' which can be used as an adjective or an adverb.

Another example could be that if the worm was a good dragon, then the adverbs suggested could be:

kindly, sweetly, innocently, generously, nicely or gently.

You could create adverb word banks for evil worms, deadly worms, ferocious worms, etc. The children could choose one of the adverbs that you have suggested, but then try to think of their own as well. As the adverbs that you have given them have been grouped according to their meaning, then the children might choose an adverb that they have never used before, but use it in the correct context because of the way that they have been introduced to the new vocabulary.

After that, the children could add any other features to their worm which might include prepositions for the places it lives in or visits. A name could be added, too, which might involve the place that the worm is from. This could be a local area dragon such as the Cardiff worm, the Edinburgh worm, the Belfast worm or the London worm.

Finally, now that all of that rich vocabulary has been gathered, the children will be ready to write their own worm descriptions. They could do this independently, or perhaps you could offer some sentence starters such as:

The worm had . . .
Its horns were . . .
On its body . . .
The claws . . .
Its wings . . .
It can . . .
It was called . . .

Once the worms have been described using noun phrases, verbs, adverbs, prepositions, etc., the children could use their writing to help them to also write a poem in the style of *The Jabberwocky*. This template gives an example of how the children could insert their own vocabulary but keeping in the same style as Lewis Carroll's famous poem.

It was _____ and the _____ _____
Did _____ and _____ in the _____:
All _____ were the _____,
And the _____ _____ _____.

'Beware the _____, my child!
The _____ that _____, the _____ that _____!
Beware the _____ bird, and shun
The _____ _____!'

Taking the _____ sword in hand:
Long time the _____ foe was sought –
So rested by the _____ tree,
And stood awhile in thought.

And, as in _____ thought the hero stood,
The _____, with _____ of _____,
Came _____ through the _____ wood,
And _____as it came!

One, two! One, two! And through and through
The _____ blade went _____!
Leaving it dead, and with its head
Went _____ back.

'And, have you slain the _____?
Come to my arms, my beamish child!
O _____ day! _____! _____!'
They both chortled in joy.

3 Monday, Tuesday (Irish)

Fairies in Ireland are said to be descended from the Tuatha de Danaan who were one of the first Celtic tribes to settle in the country. They shrank themselves using magic so that no one could find them and then went to live beneath the ground when other tribes arrived. The fairies are called Aos Sí and they are said to co-exist with humans. They are the guardians of the land, so woe betide any human that treats Ireland destructively and without respect. They live beneath fairy hills or fairy rings. Sometimes they live inside trees or under rivers or lochs and will protect their homes fiercely. They reward humans who treat the Aos Sí and their homes with respect, but punish those who do not.

Monday, Tuesday

There was once a cheerful old man called Lusmore who lived in a small village in Ireland. You could never meet such a nice old man as this one; he always had a kind word and a smile for everybody he met. He had worked hard his whole life and, as a result, his back was all hunched up on the left side. But this didn't make his mood bad. He was often seen walking up and down the high street hunched up, waving and stopping to ask people how they were.

Now, in this village there lived another old man called Jack Madden. He couldn't have been any more different. This old man was the grumpiest, meanest, rudest old man you could ever meet. He too had worked hard his whole life and, as a result, was all hunched up on the right side. This made his mood all the worse. He was often seen walking up and down the high street hunched up, grimacing and swearing at everyone he met.

One day, the cheerful old Lusmore was off walking past the high street and decided to go for a small stroll through the woods nearby. He often liked to stop and feed the birds and squirrels in those woods. He stopped, sat down on a fallen tree and was throwing nuts and seed around when all of a sudden, he heard strange singing coming from the trees beyond.

The singing went as follows:

♫ Monday . . . Tuesday ♫

then again,

♫ Monday . . . Tuesday ♫

and again,

♫ Monday . . . Tuesday ♫

Lusmore thought that this was the most beautiful singing he had ever heard. He just couldn't help himself; he just had to join in.

When the singing went,

♫ Monday . . . Tuesday ♫

the cheerful old man went,

♫ Wednesday . . . Thursday ♫

At that moment, a whole parade of fairies stepped out from the trees and stood in front of the cheerful old man. Each was no taller than a daffodil and wore sycamore-green clothes. They had long golden hair that shone in the bright sun.

One fairy wearing a golden crown skipped over to the cheerful old Lusmore and spoke:

'Ah, thank you! Thank you so much! We've been singing that song for years and we just couldn't remember the next line. Thank you again. It's a lovely cheerful tune, isn't it?'

'Erm, yes, it is!' beamed Lusmore.

'Is there something you want in return for helping me? Gold, perhaps?' asked the fairy king and, as he said this, several other fairies pulled up a mighty old box from beneath the ground. Gold glinted from inside as the fairies opened it.

'Oh, no thank you,' smiled Lusmore. 'Just seeing you happy and enjoying the song is payment enough for me.'

'There must be something I can help you with!' exclaimed the fairy king. 'What about that hunchback on your left side? I can fix that for you!'

'Ah, that would be grand! Thank you!'

With that, the fairies all began to sing a different song. A song that went,

> ♫ Lusmore! The hunch that you wore is now no more. ♫
> ♫ Look down on the floor to see it, Lusmore! ♫

Lusmore could not believe it. He stood as straight as a tower and he'd never felt better. His hunch was completely gone from his left side. He cheerfully skipped back home and could hear the fairies singing as he went.

> ♫ Monday . . . Tuesday ♫
> ♫ Wednesday . . . Thursday ♫

Lusmore was running up and down the streets of the village and shaking hands with everyone he met. He told his story a hundred times and everyone was overjoyed for the cheerful old man. Everyone, except for the grumpy old Jack Madden.

'You big fool!' he cried out to Lusmore when he heard the story. 'I'd have taken the gold *and* got my hunchback fixed too! You big fool!'

Jack Madden then bought some nuts and seeds from the local store and hobbled off into the woods. He immediately started to throw the nuts and the seeds at any animal he saw. Soon enough, all the woodland animals had scattered and were hidden, afraid of being pelted with food.

Then, all was quiet and still in the wood. Jack Madden sat down and listened.

♫ Monday . . . Tuesday ♫
♫ Wednesday . . . Thursday ♫

Jack Madden then called out:

'Friday and Saturday, and you forgot about Sunday as well, you little dafties!'

The fairies stepped out from the woods. Their faces were masks of rage. Jack Madden gulped and said:

'Erm, so I helped you with your song, like. So, erm, can I have some gold, then, or what?'

The king of the fairies frowned, then snapped his fingers. The other fairies pushed their hands beneath the ground and pulled out the mighty old box. They threw it over to Jack Madden, which nearly knocked him off his feet. But the grumpy old man didn't mind. He grinned as he greedily opened the box and stared at the gold coins inside.

The fairies then turned to walk off into the woods when Jack Madden called out, 'Hey! Wait on, you little dafties! What about me old hunchback, eh? What about fixing that, too?'

The fairies flew over and roughly rubbed at Jack Madden's back, then said, 'Get some rest, then in the morning, you'll see.'

They then fluttered away, disappearing between the trees. Jack Madden then walked off into the woods with a grin on his face, singing:

♫ Monday . . . Tuesday ♫
♫ Wednesday . . . Thursday ♫
♫ Friday . . . Saturday ♫
♫ Sunday . . . Sunday ♫

Jack Madden went to bed that night feeling very excited. He put the mighty old box on the floor next to his bed and slipped into a peaceful sleep.

His first thoughts in the morning were of his hunch. He pulled himself out of bed and, to his horror, discovered that his hunch was still there. And, even worse, now he had one on the left-hand side, too. Jack Madden kicked the mighty old box in temper. The lid swung open and inside, there were no gold coins, but only dust.

'*What*?!' bellowed Jack Madden. 'I've been tricked!'

He then stomped out of the house and into the woods, shouting insults and swearing terribly, searching for the fairies.

As soon as he arrived in the woods, the fairies flew out, disturbed by the grumpy old man's noise. They flew around him and called:

♫ Jack Madden! Jack Madden! ♫
♫ Your words came so bad in. ♫
♫ Now your life we will sadden! ♫
♫ Away, away goes Jack Madden! ♫

That grumpy old man was never seen again.

And, if you go into the woods and you hear strange singing, then watch out because the fairies reward those who do good, and may just punish those who do not.

About this story

Where did Jack Madden go? Where did the fairies take him and what did they do with him? If you do an internet search for 'Fairyland' the images are bright and colourful with rainbows, unicorns and mushroom houses. However, I suspect that where Jack went wasn't like this. Ask the children to draw where they think Jack went. Then ask them to compare their pictures with each other. How do they compare? What are the similarities and differences?

Teaching idea: Researching Fairyland

Ask the children to research Fairyland. What are the common themes? Where do the fairies live? What animals and plants are there? The children could write short descriptions based on their research.

Fairy doors are widely available and don't just have to be used outside. A door can be installed on the wall of the classroom. Somewhere high up is recommended so that the children don't just remove it and discover that it is held up with Blu Tak rather than fairy dust.

You could write letters from the fairies to your class in order to control the kind of writing you would like from them. You and your class could 'find' this tiny letter written in font size 3 on MS Word so that it looks like this:

Dear Year 2,

We are the fairies from Fairyland. People think we live in mushroom houses but we don't. Our houses are made from sticks and leaves. They are like a tent only much cosier. We have gardens where we grow our own fruits and vegetables.

It is recommended that you have a magnifying glass so that you can read what you have written.

When magnified, we can read:

> *Dear Year 2,*
>
> *We are the fairies from Fairyland. People think we live in mushroom houses but we don't. Our houses are made from sticks and leaves. They are like a tent only much cosier. We have gardens where we grow our own fruits and vegetables.*

The letter could then go on to explain other features of Fairyland. Perhaps other mythical creatures live there too such as trolls, leprechauns, giants, goblins, ogres, unicorns, firebirds or talking animals.

The children could write descriptions of daily life in Fairyland, all with suggestions from you via each letter. On one day the letter might describe the houses that the fairies live in and on another it might describe fairy school or home life, focusing on the routine of the school day or the weekend. Other details such as friends, family and pets could also be added. Food might also play an important part in the life of a fairy. On another day the weather, or perhaps some unusual events, could be described. This could lead to narrative story writing as events could unfold such as a witch who turns all the fairies into slugs, or a giant who keeps knocking down their houses, or leprechauns who keep stealing their money.

The children could write back with suggestions as to what they think could be done to help the fairies and share their ideas with each other. It is recommended in this case that you add something at the bottom of the letter, such as:

PS We do not hurt each other in Fairyland!

This may perhaps alter the children's original ideas as they are not allowed to kill these bad characters, but instead may perhaps use an alternate idea such as building a trap, trying to make friends or teaching the characters to be good. Your class could write replies to the fairies with their ideas. This might result in an ongoing dialogue between the fairies and the children that leads to more letter writing, but the stories themselves could also be written. The children could begin by describing Fairyland, moving on to outlining the problem the fairies were having and finishing with how they overcame the problem.

For older children, the letters sent might be from Jack Madden who describes where he has ended up and how he was punished.

4 The witch cats (Welsh)

Huw Llwyd was the seventh son of a seventh son, which made him a powerful magician and storyteller. He had once been a soldier, but eventually he settled by the River Cynfael in Llanrwst, which is now at the edge of Snowdonia National Park in North Wales. It was there that he studied magical books and learnt his skills of conjuring. He used these for good and helped people who needed his magic. There are many tales about him, but this story focuses on his visit to an inn where two sisters are not as they may at first seem.

The witch cats

There was once an inn on the road between Betws-y-Coed and Cerrigydrudion. It was popular with travellers, traders and musicians who were returning from Ireland, but something strange had begun to happen at the inn. People were complaining that their money went missing even though they had locked their doors and hidden their valuables. No one had entered the rooms throughout the night, so it was a complete mystery.

News of the robberies reached Huw Llwyd, the magician. He was wise and always seemed to know what to do. Huw agreed to investigate and said he would do his best to unravel the mystery. He found his old officer's uniform and dressed as a soldier with his sword in his scabbard by his belt. He then travelled to the inn where he met the two sisters who were the innkeepers.

'Good evening,' Huw smiled as he entered the inn. 'I seek a room for the night.'

'You are most welcome,' smiled one sister.

'Have you travelled far?' asked the other.

'No, not far,' answered Huw. 'I'm on my way to Ireland, though, and need to rest.'

There were very few guests that night. The sisters had made a huge pot of lamb stew and baked a large loaf of clay-pot bread. Huw and the other guests sat and ate contentedly. The sisters meanwhile told tales they had heard from previous travellers. They told stories of Prince Dyfed in the Underworld and of Math, the Lord of Gwynedd, who turned his nephews into beasts. Huw listened happily and, when he had finished his dinner, told his own stories of his travels around the world.

Finally, it was time for bed. Huw then said, 'As a soldier, I usually have the lights on all night in case I am needed. May I have enough candles to burn all night?'

The sisters agreed and sent him to his room with two handfuls of candles. Once in his room, Huw placed his clothes on the floor beside the bed and had his sword unsheathed upon the bed ready to challenge any robber. The candles were lit and Huw lay down and pretended to sleep.

Nothing happened for a while, until at last there came a soft rustling sound from the fireplace. Huw opened his eyes slightly. Through slitted eyes he could see movement upon the ashes of the cold fire. Two black cats emerged from the fireplace. They had climbed down the chimney and into his room. Their sleek, oily fur reflected the flickering candlelight and their yellow eyes scanned the room with cunning. They leapt upon Huw's clothes, pawing at the pockets. One cat then grabbed a leather string with its paw. The other cat looked on with glee. The string was drawn around a leather bag that held Huw's coins. The cat was opening the bag when Huw grabbed his sword. He swiftly struck the paw of the cat and it howled in pain. Both cats then leapt into the fireplace and disappeared up the chimney.

The next morning, Huw dressed and went downstairs for breakfast. When he arrived at his table, there was only one sister serving laverbread cakes with bacon and eggs.

'Good morning,' smiled Huw.

'Good morning to you,' said the sister. 'How did you sleep?'

'Soundly,' Huw replied. 'Where is your sister?'

'She is unwell and won't be down today.'

'What a shame. I hope she is better soon.'

Huw silently ate his breakfast. He returned to his room for his belongings, then went back downstairs to pay for his lodgings and bid farewell.

'What a shame I can't see your sister and say goodbye,' Huw said. 'I have a coin here for each of you.'

The sister's eyes lit up at the mention of money.

'Perhaps you could see my sister in her bed?' suggested the girl.

Huw agreed and was taken to the bedroom belonging to the two sisters. There were two beds and in one was the sister who was unwell.

'I'm sorry to hear you feel unwell,' Huw began. 'I had a wonderful night's sleep. Here is a coin for each of you.'

He held out the coin for each sister. The one in the bed took it with her left hand, but kept the right hand beneath the covers.

'Well, goodbye,' said Hugh while offering the first sister a handshake.

She shook hands with him, then he offered his right hand to the sister in her bed. She offered him her left hand.

'My dear girl,' smiled Huw. 'It is usual to shake hands with the right hand.'

She pulled her right hand free from the covers to reveal that it was covered in bandages. Huw shook her right hand very gently.

'I know you to be witches. I know you have used your powers to turn yourselves into cats and rob the travellers who stay here, but I am Huw Llwyd, the seventh son of a seventh son and my magic is more powerful than yours. I have drawn blood from you and your powers are now gone.'

The sister in the bed gasped when she heard this. The other sister turned to run, but Huw drew his sword and took her hand. He made another cut and the sister cried out in pain.

'No longer will you shape shift and make mischief!' Huw announced and strode out of the inn back to his home.

The two sisters didn't rob anyone ever again. They worked hard at the inn and it prospered. They became wealthy women, but often sat during the evening looking at the moon and longing to be cats once more.

About this story

The two sisters were able do something called 'transmogrify'. Transmogrification means transforming oneself in a magical and often surprising way. There are many stories of witches and wizards turning themselves and others into animals. Professor McGonagall first meets her class in the form of a cat in *Harry Potter and the Philosopher's Stone*.

Teaching idea: Turning into an animal

Ask the children to imagine that they could turn into an animal, but ensure that they tell no one what their animal is. Explain that the kind of writing they are going to do is 'showing and not telling'. One way to explain this is to say that instead of writing 'I was scared', you could write 'My heart was pounding in my chest and my hands began to shake'. That way you are showing that you are scared rather than telling the reader that you were scared.

For our writing, the children could use this same method of showing and not telling, so that after their descriptions are read aloud, the rest of the class could guess the animal that they have transmogrified into.

The children could consider how their ears, nose, mouth, etc. might change first. They could then move on to arms, legs, fingers, skin, hair, etc. If they begin with their ears, you might ask them if their ears get bigger, smaller, fall off or stay the same. You could ask them if their ears change colour or shape. Once they have described this, then the children could move on to the other body parts they have considered.

You could model some sentence starters such as:

First of all, my ears began to _____ .
Suddenly, my feet _____ .
Almost at once, my fingers _____ .
Immediately, my skin _____ .
Then, my arms _____ .
At the same time, my voice _____ .
Instantly, my eyes _____ .
At once, my nose _____ .
Next, my legs _____ .
Finally, I started to _____ .

The children could also use varied sentence openers as well as time conjunctions. Perhaps a fronted adverbial such as surprisingly, amazingly or astonishingly could be used.

In the last sentence, the children could consider what they do as their animal. Do they run, jump, play, hide, look for food, etc.?

It is important not to make the animal too easy to guess. If the children began with:

First of all, my ears began to fall into a web

or

First of all, my ears began to become covered in orange fur with black stripes on them

then the other children would guess the answer straight away.

More detailed description could be added to this writing once the ideas have been collected. So, for example, the writing could begin with:

First of all, my ears began to become brown.
Suddenly, my feet were hooves.
Almost at once, my fingers went away.
Immediately, my skin was furry.

This writing could then be expanded into:

It was all rather sudden, but first of all my small ears began to grow and become a deep brown with soft fur. Suddenly, my feet changed in the strangest way too and were now rounded and hard hooves. Almost at once, I felt amazed and terrified as my fingers went away. Immediately, I noticed that my skin was covered in smooth and sleek fur.

In this same style, the children could then describe the rest of their bodies as they transmogrify. Then they could guess which animals they have each turned into.

5 Jack and the Beanstalk (English)

There are many 'Jack' stories from England. Jack is a generic character who personifies a wild boy who longs for excitement and adventure. It is from these stories that we derive the expression 'Jack the lad' for someone of a similar nature to the fictional Jack. This story is probably the most famous Jack story. I have told it in the first person so that children can identify themselves with the character. This lends itself to the activities which follow too.

Jack and the Beanstalk

Once upon a time, when I was young, my mother and I were very poor. We did have one thing that kept us alive, though, which was our cow called Milky. We loved Milky. She gave us a bucket of milk to share between us every day.

One day, my mother said, 'It's no use. I've tried and tried, but Milky won't give any milk. She's dried up!'

'Don't be silly!' says I. 'Let me try.'

But, try as I might, there was no milk to be had.

'There's nothing for it,' said my mother. 'Go and sell Milky.'

'What?' I protested. 'We can't – she's part of the family!'

'Go and sell Milky or we'll starve!'

So off I went, mumbling and kicking at the dusty road, leading Milky towards the market. Just then, an old man stopped me and said: 'Where are you off to then, Jack?'

It's a very curious thing when someone knows your name but you don't know theirs.

'I'm off to the market to sell poor old Milky,' I replied.

'Oh, she doesn't look too well,' smiled the old man. 'You won't get much for her. I tell you what, I'll take her off your hands if you want me to.'

'In return for what?' I asked.

'These beans!' he beamed, revealing five beans in his wrinkled hand. 'Not any old beans, but magic beans that will always provide. Swap these beans for Milky and, if I'm wrong, then you come back and see me. We'll swap back.'

Now that sounded like a fair deal, so I agreed and skipped back home with the five magic beans in my pocket.

'*What?*' thundered my mother when she heard my story. 'You foolish boy, you've been tricked! Now we'll starve for sure. Get up to your room and don't come out until morning.

There'll be no tea for either of us tonight or any night. As for these *magic* beans, they are useless as you are!'

She threw them right out of the kitchen window and I went up to my room, then threw myself down on the bed. Had I been tricked? I felt terrible, but eventually I fell asleep.

In the morning, I was in shadow. I looked through the window and saw that five enormous beanstalk vines had grown from our garden where my mother had thrown the beans from the window. They intertwined one another and stretched impossibly high up into the clouds above. I opened my window and could actually touch the monstrous plant. I climbed onto the windowsill and grabbed on to one great green vine. I had to know where it led, so I began to climb.

And climb.

And climb.

Higher and higher I went right up into the clouds themselves. I emerged at a long grey road, so I hoisted myself up onto the road and saw that it led to a great castle. With a hop and a skip, I bounded off along the road. The castle was like nothing I'd ever seen before. Great grey turrets that went up so high that they made my head spin. Flags topped the turrets and waved among the stars. I whistled in awe, then walked right through the massive open door.

The first room I came to was a kitchen where a *very* tall woman was slicing a large loaf of bread.

'Morning!' I sang cheerfully. 'You wouldn't mind doing me a bit of toast would you? I've had nothing to eat since breakfast yesterday!'

The tall woman looked shocked.

'Get out of here!' she shrieked. 'My master is a giant and he'll eat you up if he sees you here!'

Suddenly there was a loud booming sound getting louder and louder still. The whole kitchen began to shake. The pots and plates quivered and quaked.

'He's here! I warned you!' the tall woman screamed. 'Get in the oven, hide there!'

I leapt into the thankfully cold oven just as the giant emerged into the kitchen.

> Fee-fi-fo-fum,
> I smell the blood of an Englishman,
> Be he alive or be he dead,
> I'll grind his bones to make my bread!

'Don't be silly!' cried the tall woman. 'You can just smell the boy you ate last night. Now sit down and eat your breakfast.'

The tall woman produced a plate of steaming cow on toast, which the giant devoured in seconds – horns, hoofs, udders and all.

'That's better!' boomed the giant. 'Now bring me my gold to count!'

The tall woman rushed out of the kitchen and returned with a wheelbarrow filled with golden coins. The giant scooped the gold up onto the table and began counting. He sorted it into piles of one hundred, then bagged each pile up.

After a while, the giant was moving slower and slower. After bagging up his seventy-second pile, he fell fast asleep with his head on the table. Before the tall woman noticed, I was gone. I sneaked out of the oven, grabbed one of the bags of gold and was out of that castle in a flash. I raced to the beanstalk and climbed down with the bag of gold securely tucked into my belt.

'Mother! Mother!' I shouted once I'd climbed in through my bedroom window. 'Come and see!'

Well, we lived on that bag of gold very comfortably for a few weeks. But money comes and money certainly goes, and soon we had spent it all.

So, one morning I decided to climb back up the beanstalk and try my luck again. I walked into the kitchen of the castle to see the tall woman bowling up a pan of porridge on the stove.

'Morning!' I sang cheerfully to her again. 'You wouldn't mind pouring me a bowl of that porridge, would you? It smells lovely!'

The tall woman looked more shocked than she had done before.

'You!' she shrieked. 'My master lost a bag of his gold the last time you were here! I should never have helped a little *thief* like you!'

'Well, it was a funny story really. Shall I tell you it?'

'Oh, yes,' cried the tall woman. 'I like a good story!'

Suddenly there was that familiar loud booming sound getting louder and louder still.

'He's here!' the tall woman screamed. 'Get in the oven. You can tell me the story later!'

I leapt into the cold oven and heard:

Fee-fi-fo-fum,
I smell the blood of an Englishman,
Be he alive or be he dead,
I'll grind his bones to make my bread!

'You're being silly again!' cried the tall woman. 'You can just smell the boy you ate yesterday afternoon. Now sit down and eat your breakfast.'

The tall woman produced a bowl of hot porridge with a roasted pig on top. The giant gobbled up the lot in seconds – snout, ears, curly tail and all.

'That's better!' boomed the giant. 'Now bring me my magic hen!'

The tall woman rushed out of the kitchen and returned with a white hen, which she put in front of him on the table. The giant said:

'Lay!'

The hen looked startled for a moment then . . . plop! . . . out popped a golden egg.

The giant chuckled and stroked the magic hen until he fell fast asleep with his head on the table. Before the tall woman could notice my escape, I was gone. I sneaked out of the oven, crept over to the table and had the magic hen under my arm in seconds. I ran to the beanstalk and climbed down one-handed with the magic hen tucked under my other arm.

'Mother! Mother!' I shouted once I'd climbed in through my bedroom window. 'Come and see this time!'

I set the hen on the kitchen table and said: 'Lay!'

Plop!

Well, we lived on the money we got from selling the golden eggs extremely comfortably. You could even say we were rich! But after a while, I began to feel curious about what else I could find in that giant's castle. So, one morning I decided to climb back up that beanstalk and try my luck for a third time. I walked into the kitchen of the castle to see the tall woman frying eggs in a pan. This time I sneaked straight past her and hid in a copper bucket behind the door of the kitchen. Suddenly, there was that familiar loud booing sound getting louder and louder still.

> Fee-fi-fo-fum,
> I smell the blood of an Englishman,
> Be he alive or be he dead,
> I'll grind his bones to make my bread!

'Do you now?' cried the tall woman. 'Well, it must be that thief and trickster who was here last time! He'll be hiding in the oven!'

The tall woman hurled open the oven only to see it empty.

'Oh, you silly giant!' she screeched. 'You can just smell the boy you ate yesterday morning.'

The tall woman then produced a plate of fried eggs with a boiled donkey on top. The giant gobbled up the lot in seconds – eyes, legs, bottom and all.

'That's better!' boomed the giant. 'Now bring me my golden harp!'

The tall woman rushed out of the kitchen and returned with a golden harp, which she put in front of him on the table. The giant said, 'Sing!'

The golden harp began to play the most beautiful music I'd ever heard. The giant listened to the golden harp until he fell fast asleep with his head on the table. Before anyone could notice I'd ever been there, I sneaked out of the bucket, crept over to the table and had the golden harp under my arm in seconds.

But the golden harp cried out, 'Help me, master! Help me! I'm being stolen away!'

The giant raised his mighty head and saw me running for the door. I ran to the beanstalk as fast as my little legs would carry me with the giant thundering after me. As I climbed down one-handed with the golden harp tucked under my arm I shouted out:

'Mother! Mother! Fetch me an axe! Quickly!'

I threw down the golden harp, looked up and saw the giant clumsily climbing down after me. I leapt down the last part of the beanstalk, grabbed the axe and began to swing it. I chopped with all my might and soon the five intertwined stalks began to creak and groan – then fall. That mighty beanstalk fell crashing down and so did the giant. His head fell first and he was dead.

My mother and I danced for joy. We'd have the golden eggs to spend all day long and the golden harp to sing to us all night long. We were happier than we had ever been all our lives.

About this story

Jack stories were told orally and are probably Norse in origin. In Norse mythology there is a similar character called Askelad, whose name means 'ash lad'. He's a lazy boy who always sits by the fire until it turns to ashes, but always seems to end up in an adventure of sorts.

Jack also features in Appalachian folklore from the United States of America. These are similar to the Jack stories from England, but with small changes to settings and characters. For example, if there was a king in the English version, the Appalachian version might have a sheriff instead.

Teaching idea: Adapting the story

We could use this model for adapting the story with the children in the classroom. In the story, the main character is Jack. The children will be the main character in their own narrative. It will be a first-person, past-tense narrative. The other characters could be of their own choosing. Instead of Jack's mother, the children could choose a different family member or someone altogether new. It could be their friends, either imaginary or real.

The giant character could be a monster, a Big Bad Wolf, a witch, troll, ogre or other traditional tale villain. The children could design and describe their new character. You might offer some incorrect adjective examples such as:

cute, kind, friendly, nice, beautiful, loving, caring, lovely, handsome, awesome, epic, good, etc.

Then the children have to write opposite adjectives of their own, choosing to describe their own villainous characters.

Instead of selling a cow called Milky, perhaps the children could have to sell a different animal such as Inky the Octopus, Freddie the Fly or Digger the Dog. It's a good idea to give the animal a task like Milky giving milk so that the narrative structure can remain the same. For example, Inky the Octopus used to give ink so that the children could write stories. Freddie the Fly used to eat up all the mess in the house. Digger the Dog used to dig up vegetables for them to eat. But then the animal stops doing what it is meant to do and needs to be sold. The selling could take place at a market or the children could choose a different place.

The old man with the magic beans could then be changed. It could be an old woman such as a witch or a different character entirely such as a princess, wizard, goblin or leprechaun.

The five magic beans could become five magic seeds, flowers, shells, bones, twigs, scales, etc. These could then grow something instead of a beanstalk such as a tree, mountain, tower, volcano, portal, bridge, river, etc. This then leads to somewhere else where the villainous character lives. Instead of a giant in a castle, it could be a monster in a cave, a wolf in a forest, a witch in a hut, a troll in graveyard or an ogre in a swamp, etc.

The last changes to be made are to the three things that Jack collected from the giant's castle. Instead of golden coins, magic hen and talking harp, the children could choose three different things. They could start with something valuable like coins, but make it pearls, diamonds, opals, rubies, emeralds or sapphires. The second object could be a money-making pet like the golden egg-laying hen. Or perhaps the animal could do something useful for the children, such as a goat that makes pizza, a cat that does homework or a fish that can clean their room.

Now the children have all the tools to tell their own Jack and the Beanstalk style story. They would need to add for description, but the basic structure of the story could begin like this:

> Once upon a time, I lived with my best friend Adeen. We had an octopus that used to squirt out ink so that we could write stories. But Inky the Octopus dried up, so Adeen told me to sell Inky to Aldi and get some money in return.
>
> On my way to Aldi, I met a witch who offered me five magic twigs. I swapped Inky for the sticks and went home to tell Adeen. She went crazy and threw the sticks out of the window!
>
> The next morning the sticks had turned into a giant tree. I decided to climb the tree to see what was at the top. When I finally reached the top, I saw a stinky swamp in the clouds. I explored the stinky swamp and realised it was the home of an evil, gruesome, nasty, mean and ugly ogre.
>
> The ogre sat on the floor and began to count his diamonds into bags. There were a thousand of them! Eventually the ogre fell asleep. I took the bag of diamonds and ran off down the tree to show Adeen.

The story could then go on to describe the second and third object, with an ending that the children choose themselves. Maybe they chop down the tree or explode the mountain with TNT. The children could be given a couple of examples, but essentially make the decision themselves.

It would be beneficial for the children to orally tell the story first before writing it down. It doesn't have to make complete sense as this is a fantasy using traditional tale elements.

6 The rich lord's wife (Welsh)

Wales has a long and celebrated history of writing, but oral storytelling is something that predates this. Welsh is a Celtic language and has been spoken since the sixth century. It is one of the oldest European languages and many Welsh people are thankfully keeping that language alive. This story is a typical example of Welsh storytelling and the poem sums up the tradition rather well.

> Dwedai hen ŵr llwyd o'r gornel:
> 'Gan fy nhad mi glywais chwedel;
> A chan ei daid y clywsai yntau,
> Ac ar ei ôl mi gofiais innau.'

'Baled yr Hen ŵr o'r Coed', 18g

> An old grey man in the corner said:
> 'I heard my father tell a tale;
> He heard it from his grandfather,
> And I remembered it from him.'

'The Ballad of the Old Man of the Woods', 18th century

The rich lord's wife

Once there lived a rich old lord who lived in a huge castle. He owned many acres of land, wore fine clothes, had money in the bank, a pet octopus, you name it – he had it. But he was lonely, for although he had a great many possessions, he had no wife.

One day, he was out riding on his fine stallion when he passed a poor farmer's house. Now this farmer lived on the lord's land, so the lord thought nothing at all of simply riding his horse through the poor farmer's back garden to look at the many flowers that bloomed there. As the rich lord did so, he noticed the poor farmer's daughter cutting some flowers and placing them in a basket. She was young and beautiful.

He brought his horse alongside her and said: 'Good day to you, my pretty. I was just wondering, perhaps you would consider becoming my wife?'

He flashed a dazzling smile and winked at her as he said this.

'What?' she spluttered. 'I'm not going to marry you. You're old – and you're ugly. No way!'

And with that she stomped off into the house. The rich lord was in a terrible temper. Nobody had ever said no to him before! He rode his horse round to the front of the poor farmer's house, slid down from his saddle and hammered at the door.

'Erm, yes, my lord? Can I help you?' asked the poor farmer as he answered the door.

'Yes, you can!' boomed the rich lord. 'I just asked your daughter to marry me – and she said no! Is it not a great honour for me to propose to your daughter?'

'Indeed it is, sir,' replied the poor farmer.

'And would she not be rich beyond her wildest dreams?' demanded the rich lord.

'Indeed she would, sir,' answered the poor farmer.

'And is it not right that she should agree to marry me then, eh?' enquired the rich lord menacingly.

'Erm, well, I suppose it is, sir.'

'Right, then!' bellowed the rich lord. 'You have just promised me your daughter's hand in marriage!'

'But . . . ,' began the poor farmer.

'No "buts", man! A promise is a promise,' said the rich lord, shaking his hands in the air and walking back to his stallion. 'I will set the wedding for one week's time at the church. And your daughter had better be there!'

With that the rich lord steered his horse away and sped off to his castle.

A week later and the wedding was prepared. The church was decorated with flowers from top to bottom. The reception would take place in the field next to the church where a gigantic marquee stood. The tables sagged under the weight of the food and the drink. People were dressed in their finest clothes. Everyone in the land had turned up to witness the marriage and join in the celebration – everyone, that is, except for the poor farmer's daughter. The rich lord grew more and more impatient as he stood waiting inside the church. At last, he clapped his hands and sent for his messenger.

'Messenger!' he bellowed. 'Go to the poor farmer's house and demand what I have been promised!'

'Right away, sir!' replied the messenger and he sped off as fast as his feet could carry him.

When he arrived at the poor farmer's house, breathless and panting, he knocked at the door.

The poor farmer's daughter answered the door and said, 'Yes? Can I help you?'

'Right,' said the messenger. 'The rich lord says that he wants what's been promised to him.'

'Oh, I see,' replied the poor farmer's daughter, thinking quickly. 'He's talking about a horse! There's a female horse he's been wanting from us. You know – a mare for his stallion. She's down round the back of the garden. Help yourself!'

With that, the messenger went round the back of the garden, untied the horse and led her to the church as fast as he could. He then tethered her to a tree and rushed to tell the rich lord he had been successful.

'I've done it!' the messenger said. 'She's outside.'

'Right, then,' beamed the rich lord. 'Take her to my castle and lead her into my mother's bedroom.'

'What?' gasped the messenger.

'You heard me. Now do it,' answered the rich lord gruffly.

'What if she struggles when I'm getting her up the stairs?' asked the messenger, rather bemused.

'Then get some friends to help you. Now go!' demanded the rich lord.

So the messenger untied the horse and led her to the rich lord's castle. With some help, he got the horse up the stairs and into the bedroom. He then rushed back to the church and said, 'I've done it! She's in your mother's bedroom.'

'Excellent,' grinned the rich lord. 'Now dress her in fine silks and exquisite velvet.'

'*What*?!' spluttered the messenger.

'You heard me. Now do it!'

'OK, then,' said the messenger, as again he sped back to the castle. He then dressed the horse in the finest gown he had ever seen and rushed back to the church.

'I've done it. She's wearing a fine gown!' the messenger said.

'Marvellous,' beamed the rich lord. 'Now give her some jewellery and some make-up.'

'*W-what*?!' stammered the messenger.

'You heard me. Now do it!'

'OK, then,' the messenger replied as he sped back to the castle. When he got there, he put some lipstick and some eyeliner on the horse. Then he put on some earrings and a necklace. Then at last he rushed back to the church.

'I've done. She's all made up,' the messenger said.

'Superb,' leered the rich lord. 'Now bring her to me – I wish to marry her!'

'*W-w-what*?!' gabbled the messenger.

'You heard me. Now do it!'

'OK, then,' shrugged the messenger as he sped back to the castle. He then led the horse down the stairs, through the doors and along the road to the church.

When the messenger arrived, he flung open the church doors and the whole of the congregation saw the horse in the wedding dress. They all laughed and laughed and laughed.

The horse stared at the rich lord.

The rich lord stared at the horse.

The horse saw how old and ugly the rich lord was and neighed loudly, then bolted from the church as fast as it could.

'*Neigggghhhh*!'

Outside the church, the rich lord's stallion saw the horse in the wedding dress and fell in love instantly. The stallion and the mare lived happily ever after.

As for the rich lord? That grumpy old miser never did find love or happiness.

About this story

Early storytellers would have told tales of Celtic gods and goddesses. The first recording of this was a collection of eleven tales known as the *Mabinogion*. This was written some time between the eleventh and thirteenth centuries. However, the stories would have been told orally a long time before this. The story above shows a shift in style and formality from the earlier tales. It is a good example of the wit and humour used in more modern storytelling set in contemporary society.

Teaching idea: Describing characters

We could use this story to describe the two main characters whose appearance and personality are at polar opposites to each other. Ask the children to sit with a partner with whiteboards and pens. The children could then make a list of adjectives for one character on one whiteboard. One child could work as the scribe, with both contributing to the list. Then, the other child could be the scribe and list the adjectives describing the other character. The first list of adjectives could be used to help as the children think of opposite adjectives. For example, if the girl is wise, beautiful and cunning, then the lord could be old, ugly and foolish.

The children could then work individually and select their favourite adjectives to create similes by comparing them to other things that could be described as similar in description. Animal similes would work well for this activity. For example, the girl could be as wise as an owl, as beautiful as a peacock or as cunning as a fox. The lord could be as old as a dinosaur, as ugly as a spider or as foolish as a donkey. But the similes don't have to be limited to animals. The girl could be as wise as King Solomon, as beautiful as a painting or as cunning as a puzzle. The lord could be as old as time, as ugly as a nightmare or as foolish as a hat made from cheese.

Once children are able to use similes effectively, metaphors can be explained and written, too. A simile compares one thing to another, but a metaphor says that something is another thing. Metaphors compare two unlike things, but says that one thing *is* another. So, the girl could be a flash of dazzling light, suggesting she is bright and clever, or she could be a rainbow, suggesting she is pretty. On the other hand, the lord could be a blunt knife, suggesting he is not useful, or he could be a nightmare, suggesting he is difficult to deal with.

Another kind of figurative language technique is hyperbole. This means to exaggerate and is something that children frequently do without realising that it is a descriptive technique they can employ in their writing. So, when they say things like, 'I've told you a thousand times' or 'I've walked a million miles', they are using hyperbole. The children could add hyperbole to their similes and metaphors by exaggerating them. For example, the girl who was as cunning as a fox and had outsmarted every farmer in the world, or she could be a dazzling rainbow that arcs over the whole world for everyone to see. The lord could be as old as an ancient dinosaur that had fossilised millions of years ago, or he could be a nightmare sent directly from hell.

Another kind of figurative language that could be used is pathetic fallacy. This is where the mood of nature, such as the weather, matches the mood and personality of the characters. This can be combined with metaphor, so we could describe the girl and the lord as types of weather. For example, the girl could be a ray of sunshine that shone brightly and the lord could be a grumbling raincloud that darkened the sky wherever he went.

We could also use alliteration, where there is repetition of the initial sound in a word. This can be overused, though, so we could ask the children to use only two or three same-sound words in any given combination. If they wrote, 'The gentle and generous girl was gleefully glad when she gallantly glided over the gloriously grassy landscape', this begins to sound ridiculous. So, being sparing is a must with alliteration. Instead, we could describe the girl as bold and brave, or clever and courageous, whereas the lord could be grimly gruesome or horrifically horrid.

By now, the children should have a range of figurative language descriptions that they can use to describe either one or both of the characters from the story.

7 The unicorn (Scottish)

In Celtic myths and legends, the unicorn is a symbol of purity, innocence and healing. Stories of unicorns date back further than the Ancient Greeks. Aristotle, the Greek philosopher, wrote about what unicorns looked like and described them as 'one-horned donkeys' and he believed that they originated in India. Whatever the origin, the unicorn is the official animal of Scotland and was chosen by King Robert III in the 1300s. It is now on the Scottish royal coat of arms and remains a symbol of nobility and power. This story shows the unicorn's power to cure any poison, even when it comes from the devil himself.

The unicorn

Long ago in Scotland, all the animals lived in perfect harmony. The cat and the dog were the best of friends. The fox and the mouse shared stories every night. The deer and the wolf played games together. They lived like a huge happy family.

Scotland itself was the most beautiful home the animals could ever wish for. Wild flowers bloomed and the trees blossomed. Huge mountains glowed purple and sandy beaches glittered golden.

The animals would gather together by a huge loch at sunrise and at sunset to drink and talk. In the day, they would watch the sun rise together and in the evening, they would watch the sun set and see the lush green landscape glow red, orange and yellow before turning blue and purple. The white light of the moon would guide them home and each would sleep blissfully looking forward to their next day.

But something had sneaked into Scotland at night. It had left its home of Eden. It was the serpent. The serpent was a creature of evil. It loved nothing better than to spoil beautiful things. It loved nothing better than to watch things burn, rot, wither. It watched with jealousy and rage as it saw the animals living together so peacefully.

So the serpent slithered and slimed its way towards the loch once all the animals had left and had fallen asleep. It stared at its own reflection in the water. It hated what it saw. It hated itself even more than it hated others. It dipped its tail into the loch and ripples distorted its features. Poison dripped from its tail into the loch. The poison spread across the surface, then mixed with the pure water. It poured all its hate and loathing out, and the loch turned black. The serpent then slithered off to cause more mischief elsewhere.

The next morning the animals gathered around the loch. The stench rising in clouds of green mist was revolting. The animals became scared. They knew that if they drank from the lake, they would die. They ran and hid.

The day turned to night. The night turned to day. The animals howled and moaned. They roared and groaned. Their thirst was too much to bear. Their suffering could be heard all over Scotland. One of the animals was unlike the others. This animal drank from a loch on top of a tall mountain in the Highlands of the north. It had remained hidden from all, but when it heard the howling and moaning of suffering, it came down from the mountain. It came down to help. This was the unicorn. It was a glowing white horse with a horn that twisted and turned from its forehead.

The unicorn trotted slowly in the light of the moon to the loch. It sang a song so beautiful that all the other animals stopped their crying and shouting to listen. They all walked, padded and crept towards the poisoned loch. They saw the unicorn glowing in the white moonlight.

Once all the animals were gathered, the unicorn stopped singing and slowly lowered its horn into the water. Gently, the white horn broke the surface of the black water and was submerged from its tip to its base. The lake began to clear. The water turned from a murky black to crystal clear. The unicorn raised its head away from the water and took a few steps backwards.

The animals all eagerly stepped towards the lake and drank. They drank and drank until their bellies were bursting. They all smiled at each other and then turned to the unicorn, but the creature had gone. It had trotted away into the Highlands of Scotland where it still lives today, hidden from view by most. But some lucky ones have seen it. Perhaps you are one of those fortunate folks.

The unicorn waits, for if the serpent were ever to return, the unicorn will always be there as the guardian of Scotland.

About this story

After hearing the story above, Queen Elizabeth I of England used to drink from a cup made from a unicorn horn as she believed that it would protect her from poisoning. The cup was actually made from a narwhal horn as, along with dragons, centaurs and mermaids, the unicorn is a mythical creature, meaning that it does not exist despite what we might wish for. Many mythical creatures combine animals to create new hybrid creatures. The Minotaur is part-man and part-bull, the Chimera combines a lion, snake and goat, and the Cockatrice is a snake, deer and chicken combination. Scotland has other mythical creatures such as Kelpies, which are water horses that can turn into humans. There is also the Wulver, which has the body of a man and the head of a wolf, among others.

Teaching idea: Combining animals

Ask the children to choose animals that can be combined together. An easy start would be a snake's body, then other features could be added such as a crab's claws, shark's head, scorpion's sting, etc. Or you could use a set of dice and a 'monster maker' like this one:

Your monster will have the head of a . . .

1	2	3	4	5	6
crocodile	shark	lion	dragon	snake	eagle

Your monster will have the body of a . . .

1	2	3	4	5	6
wolf	vulture	giraffe	horse	bear	monkey

Your monster will have the arms of a . . .

1	2	3	4	5	6
gorilla	T-Rex	tiger	dog	crab	octopus

Your monster will have the legs of a . . .

1	2	3	4	5	6
chicken	jellyfish	zebra	cat	pig	elephant

Your monster will have the tail of a . . .

1	2	3	4	5	6
lizard	fish	skunk	fox	squirrel	scorpion

There are flip books that combine animals, which could be useful as examples, and the Switch Zoo website and app could also be used. Once the children have designed their own mythical creature, they could then name it by combining parts of the animals' names they have used. However, it is best to use just two or three of the animals chosen, otherwise the names become unpronounceable. For example, if they have combined a hedgehog with a dinosaur, fish and zebra, it could be called 'Zish-Hog-Rex', 'Dinohish' or 'Hedgesaur'.

The unicorn has the power to heal and get rid of poison. It is usually a good mythical creature, but there are examples of bad unicorns such as in the story of *Herr Fix-It-Up* by the Brothers Grimm and *The Evil Unicorn of Doom* by Adam Bushnell. Ask the children to decide if their creature is good or bad. This might determine what power their creature will have. The Minotaur was super strong, the Chimera could breathe fire and the Cockatrice could petrify others, meaning it could turn them to stone. The creature the children have designed may have telekinesis powers, be able to walk through walls or control time. The power could be used to help or to heal.

The children could then begin to add more information to their creatures, such as deciding where it lives, what it eats, the noises it makes, its height, length, weight, top speed, age, threat level, intelligence, strength, weakness, etc.

Top Trump style cards could be made to compare each child's creature and a class book could be created to share the work.

Once all the detailed information has been gathered, then non-chronological reports could be written about the creatures. Key features of this style of writing should be identified, such as writing in the third person, in the present tense or past tense if now extinct, and each feature could be written in non-chronological order with a clear, factual style. There should be a heading, opening statement and subheadings with each paragraph. Other features could include bullet points, different font sizes, tables, diagrams, photographs, pictures and maps to add more information. This provides clarity and also breaks up the text. Technical language and specialist words should also be encouraged, so rather than saying 'meat eater', the word 'carnivore' could be used. Other vocabulary such as predator, herbivore, habitat, symbiotic and diet could also be used in the correct context here.

8 Tattercoats (English)

The 'Cinderella' story that is so familiar to us is the French version of the story. There are many different Cinderella stories from around the world. She is known as 'Rough Face Girl' in Native American myths, 'Yeh-Shen' in China and 'Nyasha' in Africa. In the UK there is 'Cinderlad' from Ireland, 'Rashin Coatie' from Scotland, 'The Little Sinder Girl' from Wales and 'Tattercoats' from England. It is the English version that is described here and was originally retold by Joseph Jacobs in his book More English Fairy Tales, *first published in 1894.*

Tattercoats

There was once a rich man who lived with his wife and three daughters in a large house near the royal palace. It was the rich man's birthday and he had invited all his friends from near and far to his house for a great feast. The rich man was having a wonderful time. He ate lots of food and drank far too much wine. Towards the end of the night he was very drunk. He stood up, wobbling.

'Hic! My daughters! Tell me how much you love me!' he said loudly.

'Well, Daddy,' began the eldest daughter. 'I love you more than the whole world!'

'Hic! Lovely!' smiled the rich man.

'Oh, Daddy,' said the middle daughter. 'I love you more than life itself!'

'Hic! Marvellous!' beamed the rich man.

'Well,' began the youngest daughter as she looked around the room. 'I love you more than . . .'

'Hic! More than what?' smiled the rich man.

The youngest daughter noticed how much everyone was enjoying their food. She realised that it was all the herbs and spices that made the food tasty.

'More than what?' the rich man asked again, becoming impatient.

'More than . . . more than . . . food loves herbs and spices!' the youngest daughter said, smiling.

'More than food loves herbs and spices?!' the rich man bellowed. '*More than food loves herbs and spices?!* I don't think you love me at all! Get out! Get out of my house! Hic!'

The youngest daughter burst into tears and ran off into the night. She was walking and crying, crying and walking for a long time. She was shivering as the night was so cold and all she had on was her party dress. She began to pull up weeds that grew along the path. When she had armfuls of these weeds, she sat down on the soft grass and began plaiting them together. She made a whole coat of weeds. She put the coat on and pulled the hood over her head. She then made her way further along the path until she reached the palace of the king and queen. She knocked at the door and it was instantly opened by the royal butler.

'Yes?' the butler said. 'What can I do for you?'

'I'm homeless, cold and hungry. I need a place to live. I'll wash, cook, clean. I'll do anything you need me to. Please can I stay here?'

'We always need new servants here. You can work in the kitchens in the basement,' said the butler.

'Thank you so much!' beamed the youngest daughter.

She cooked the most delicious dinners in that palace. Everyone loved the youngest daughter's food. It was all the herbs and spices she used that made them so delicious. She became known as 'Tattercoats' because she never took off her coat made from weeds.

One day, the butler burst into the kitchen.

'There's to be a ball! A feast and a dance, right here in the palace tonight!' he announced.

The whole kitchen bustled with excitement.

'The king and queen have decided that the royal prince should marry. The ball is for him to choose a wife! We are all invited – every one of us.'

There was a loud cheer and everyone began to prepare for the ball. Food was made, drinks were poured and every person in the palace put on their finest clothes. Only the youngest daughter didn't change. Her outfit was always the same.

'Are you coming to the ball, Tattercoats?' asked the butler.

'No,' answered the youngest daughter. 'I have nothing to wear.'

The butler shrugged his shoulders and went upstairs to help out at the party.

The ball began boldly with trumpets and cheering. The youngest daughter could hear the noise of talking, laughing and dancing above her. Eventually, her curiosity got the better of her and she crept upstairs and peered into the ballroom to see everyone in their finest clothes.

When she saw the prince of the palace she felt her heart pounding. He was so handsome! She had to get a closer look, so she let the coat of weeds fall to the ground and stepped into the ballroom wearing her party dress.

When the prince saw her, he gasped. 'Wow, I've never seen *you* before! Do you want to dance?'

The youngest daughter smiled and they danced the night away.

When the clock struck midnight, twelve chimes rang out. The youngest daughter was having the best time ever, but she knew that she had to be up early the next morning to make everyone their breakfast in the palace. She didn't want the prince to know that she was a servant, so she simply said:

'Well, I must go now. Goodbye!'

Then she rushed out of the door, put her coat of weeds back on and went to the kitchen.

The next morning the prince was love-struck. He sent out knights on quests to find the youngest daughter, but nobody knew who the mysterious girl was. The king and queen could take no more of the prince's constant moaning for her. They decided to hold another ball to see if the mysterious girl would appear again.

Sure enough, as the ball was in full swing, the youngest daughter crept up from the kitchen. She left her coat of weeds outside the ballroom and walked over to the prince. He was delighted! They spent another night dancing and laughing with each other. But when the twelve chimes rang out, the youngest daughter knew she had to leave. She said farewell and rushed out of the ballroom, collecting her coat of weeds as she went.

The next day, the prince was worse than before. He moaned and wailed. He pined and whined.

'If I don't see that girl again, I shall die!' he announced.

So a third ball was held. For a third time the youngest daughter entered the party late after leaving her coat of weeds outside. For a third time, she and the prince danced the night away. And, for a third time, she left the party at midnight.

The prince was worse than ever the next day. He took to his bed as he was so ill. He became worse and worse day by day.

The youngest daughter was in the kitchen preparing lunch for the palace. The butler arrived and said, 'It's no use! We've tried everything!'

'What's wrong?' asked the youngest daughter.

'The prince is on his deathbed! If we can't find who this mysterious woman he's been dancing with is, then I'm sure he will die!' he answered.

The youngest daughter gasped and said, 'I'll take the prince some vegetable soup – that will make him feel better!'

'Soup?' cried the butler. 'Soup won't help this!'

'It's worth a try,' smiled the youngest daughter. 'But I must take the soup to him *myself*.'

The butler reluctantly agreed and the youngest daughter set off up the large staircase and into the prince's room. She put a tray with the bowl of soup on top next to his bed and cheerfully said, 'Here you are!'

'I know that voice!' gasped the prince.

He leapt from his bed.

'Is that you under that coat of weeds?' he asked.

The youngest daughter let the coat of weeds fall to the ground.

'It is!' exclaimed the prince. 'I love you! Let's get married!'

'OK!' smiled the youngest daughter.

The wedding preparations were made straight away. The king and queen were delighted that their son was feeling better and thought that the youngest daughter was lovely. Everyone in the land was invited to the wedding party, even the youngest daughter's parents. The youngest daughter asked for her wedding dress to have a long veil over it so that nobody could see her face. She also asked that the food served at the party should contain no herbs and spices.

All was ready.

At the party the wedding guests ate their food, but it wasn't very tasty. It was boring and tasteless. The rich man, his wife, his eldest daughter and his middle daughter chewed the food carefully. Suddenly, the rich man stood up and exclaimed:

'This food is terrible!'

Everyone gasped.

'I now understood what my youngest daughter meant! *Food does love herbs and spices*! What have I done? I threw my youngest daughter out of the house and she loves me best of all!'

Just then, the youngest daughter pulled the veil away from her face.

'Daddy!' she shouted.

'Daughter!' he replied.

They rushed to each other and began hugging. Then the whole family had a great group hug. The rich man's family and the royal family became the best of friends. The youngest daughter and the prince were the happiest couple you could imagine and they all lived happily ever after.

About this story

This version of the story has no wicked stepsisters, but follows a similar narrative path to the French version made so famous by Disney. Instead of Cinderella being dressed in soot-covered rags, Tattercoats wears a coat of weeds.

Nature clothing is also worn by the Green Man and the Green Woman, who were the spirit of nature personified in Celtic and Anglo-Saxon mythology. Monks from Anglo-Saxon times carved the Green Man and the Green Woman into stone and wood inside churches and cathedrals all over the United Kingdom. These images were to lure local pagan people into the holy places with a familiar figure. The druid Celts prayed to the Green Man or Green Woman to bring successful harvests in the autumn and abundant fruit in the spring.

Teaching idea: The Green Man and the Green Woman

The children could be shown examples of the Green Man and the Green Woman from books and online. Point out the nature clothing they are wearing. Other examples of similar characters are Groot from *Guardians of the Galaxy* and Treebeard from *The Lord of the Rings*. Games Workshop have a series of characters called Sylvaneth that mimic the style of the Green Man and the Green Woman. Once the children are familiar with this style of character, they could be taken outside and make collages, using natural materials, of these Green Man and Green Woman characters. Ask the children to work in groups and collect items such as twigs, leaves, petals, bark, moss, grass, berries, etc. They could make their own versions of a Green Man and a Green Woman wearing natural clothing like Tattercoats. They could use gnarled and twisted branches and roots for hair on a Green Man, or garlands of flowers for hair on a Green Woman. Each character could be wearing a dress, a suit, a skirt, trainers, boots, trousers, track suits, a swimming costume or a bikini, all made from natural materials. These could be photographed and later described when the children are back in the classroom.

You could label an image of a Green Man and a Green Woman on the board as an example. Model descriptive phrases such as:

- gnarled and knotted branches;
- smooth, sleek and shiny;
- deep, emerald-green moss;
- rough grass like vicious spines;
- soft grass of feathery tendrils;

- pungent yet pleasant aroma;

- heavy, earthy scent;

- heavy bark like armour plating;

- a labyrinth of twisted sticks;

- weeds and vines intertwined into tight knots.

Encourage the children to write their own descriptive phrases. Your examples and their own writing could then be turned into sentences. Encourage the children to include three of their five senses in their descriptions.

9 The leprechaun (Irish)

Leprechauns are known all over the world but originate from Irish folklore. Some consider them to be like fairies and part of the Tuatha Dé Danaan, but others believe that leprechaun stories were told by the first natives to the country and predate any Celtic origin. Unlike fairies, leprechauns are solitary creatures who wear green and love to make mischief. The name is said to come from 'leath brogan', which means 'shoe-maker'; others believe it derives from the word 'luchorpán', which means 'small body'. The shoe-making and small body attributes are now synonymous with leprechaun folklore, as is their mischievous nature and love of trickery and riddles. The following narrative is a combination of three separate leprechaun stories into one to show all parts of the leprechaun legend.

The leprechaun

Roisin was sitting by the fire listening to her grandfather telling stories of the Tuatha Dé Danaan, the first tribes to settle in Ireland. She loved the stories of the battles against the Firbolgs, another Celtic tribe. But in the Battle of Moytura, the Tuatha Dé Danaan were victorious. Roisin clapped with glee hearing of the clash of swords, spears and shields in the storytelling.

'Right, come on now,' said her mother. 'I need some help.'

Roisin groaned and protested, but she didn't mind helping her mother really.

'What shall I do?' she asked.

'Go and gather some fruit for me, please.'

Gathering a trug woven with willow, she set off away from the house and towards the woods.

'Watch out for the little folk!' her mother called after her.

Fairies? Roisin wasn't scared of them. If she met a fairy, then she would be kind and respectful; in return, they might give her a reward like a sword made from gold. She might even meet the goddess Danu who flies with the wind. Roisin was lost in a world of stories as she entered the woods.

The bright bark of the silver birch trees that lined the outside of the woods had glowed in the sunlight, but Roisin was now immersed in a gloomy chill. She ducked under low boughs and stepped skilfully over knotted tangles of roots. Spiderweb strands stroked her skin as she passed ivy-strangled trunks. The smell of earthy soil was immense and there was a taste of fungus that was both bitter and sweet. Her eyes darted from the greens and browns until she saw a cluster of bright red. Her feet flattened some trailing ferns as she approached the berries. Her teeth popped the skin of one and the dark juice was sweet, ripe and delicious. She filled the trug and moved on to another part of the woods.

A huge oak tree with thick roots was surrounded by smaller, more spindly trees. The oak tree stifled the sunlight for the smaller ones. Leaves and bracken crunched under Roisin's feet and then she noticed a trail of smoke that drifted on the air. It was coming from the other side of the tree. She tried to make her approach less obvious. She tiptoed slowly and carefully over the forest floor and peered around the vast tree.

Sitting with his back against the tree was a very small man. It could not have been a child as the man had a thick, long beard and smoked a pipe. The man was wearing green trousers and a jacket with a brown leather apron over the top. On his head was a green cocked hat that sat at a strange angle. He had the sole of a shoe in one hand and in the other a grooving tool that he used to shape the sole. He whistled a merry tune as he worked. Roisin watched him hypnotically. The man had a variety of tools in his leather apron that he deftly swapped depending on the next job he moved on to. Soon, he was hammering little nails into the sole, attaching it to a tiny, pointed leather shoe he had crafted, all the while puffing on his pipe.

Roisin had been watching for such a long time that she shifted her weight from one foot to another. There was a cracking sound as a twig broke beneath her feet. The man looked up and leapt to his feet in fright.

'Don't be alarmed,' said Roisin with a smile. 'I bid you a very good day, sir. And what a beautiful shoe you have made. Who is it for?'

The man looked at the shoe in his hand as if noticing it for the first time.

'It's for the fairy folk,' he replied with a wry smile. 'They do wear out their shoes quickly with all that dancing.'

'They are lucky to have such a craftsman to make their shoes,' Roisin said.

The man grinned widely. He seemed delighted with the compliment.

'They pay me well with gold.'

'As they should for such beautiful work.'

The grin was now a beaming smile that revealed gleaming white teeth. The man leapt to his feet and put his tools into his apron. The shoe was carefully placed onto some soft leaves.

'What's your name?' he asked.

'Roisin. I'm delighted to meet you.'

'As I am with you. What are you doing in these woods?'

'Collecting berries for my mother.'

The man took the pipe out of his mouth and pointed it at the girl.

'You're good to your mother?'

Roisin nodded.

'You listen to what she says?'

She nodded again.

'What do they say about the fairy folk?'

'My grandfather tells me stories about them. You should always treat them with respect. They are older and wiser than us mortals.'

The man clapped his hands with glee.

'Your grandfather is a storyteller?'

Roisin nodded a third time.

'I like you,' the man said. 'I'll tell you what – answer three riddles and you might just get some gold.'

Roisin loved riddles. She and her grandfather swapped them by the fireside most evenings along with the stories. She smiled at the man and looked on with wide eyes and an eager anticipation.

'What goes up and can never go down?'

Roisin's brow furrowed. She stared at the floor, lost in thought for a few moments. Then she snapped her eyes back to the man with a smile upon her face.

'Your age!' she announced.

The man gripped his pipe with his teeth and clapped his hands.

'Correct!' he said and did a little jig. 'Next one.'

Roisin's expression was a mask of determination.

'What has to be broken before you can use it?'

The girl looked up at the trees this time with eyes squinted and her nose wrinkled. She remained motionless like that, then looked back at the man.

'An egg?' she asked inquisitively.

The man clapped again.

'Clever girl. Last one.'

Roisin took a step forward and readied herself as if she was preparing for a race. She held her breath while she waited for the last riddle. Her mind was tumbling around this way and that. She tried to focus her attention on the here and now and not think of the gold that she might just get. She tried not to think of what her mother and grandfather would say if she returned with leprechaun gold. She shook her head and stared intently at the man.

'What belongs to you but is used by others?'

With eyes boring into the ancient oak tree, Roisin was a statue in the woods. Her mind raced, but her body was frozen solid. Then she did a little jump off the floor and clapped her hands.

'Your name!'

The man also clapped with delight.

'You solved my three riddles!' he declared. 'Good on you!'

Roisin beamed with joy. She looked at the man with eager anticipation.

'You'll be wanting that gold then, eh?' he asked.

'Yes please!'

'You can find my gold at the end of the next rainbow, you see.'

With that, the man collected his shoes and walked off around the tree. Roisin followed him but he had gone. He had disappeared to wherever he lived and could not be followed by mortals. Roisin didn't mind, though. She would be rich! Collecting her trug, she ran home to her family to tell them what had happened.

On the way home, it began to rain. It was only a summer shower and it soon passed but then, as the sky cleared, a beautiful rainbow arched its way across the sky. Roisin gasped. There it was! The gold would be waiting for her at the end!

She dropped the trug and ran off, chasing the rainbow. She ran and ran and ran. She ran until she could run no more. Then she ran some more. The sky darkened and the rainbow disappeared.

Roisin trudged the many miles back home in the darkness and gloom. She had lost her chance to get the leprechaun's gold. She had failed her mother and grandfather.

It was after midnight when Roisin reached her house. Her mother was on the doorstep with a lantern calling her name. Her grandfather stood beside her with his face a knot of worry.

'There you are!' her mother called and raced towards her.

'Where have you been?' asked her grandfather.

Her mother helped her inside and Roisin sat by the fire warming her cold bones. With a few tears she told her story. Her grandfather nodded.

'Dear child,' he said. 'Don't you know there is no end to a rainbow?'

'He tricked me?' asked Roisin with wide eyes and a heavy heart.

She went to bed exhausted and tearful. She felt foolish and cheated. Sleep found her at last in the darkness of her room.

In the morning, Roisin's mother woke her up with a shake and a shout.

'Come and see!'

Roisin groaned and slipped out from the bed. Her grandfather had the front door wide open and grinned with excitement.

'Look!' he said, pointing to the porch.

There were three pairs of exquisite shoes waiting for them.

'A gift for your three answers to the riddles!' her mother said.

The leprechaun had rewarded Roisin's cleverness. It wasn't gold, but Roisin was grateful for the shoes. Perhaps they would lead her to the gold when the next rainbow appeared!

About this story

Riddles come in many forms and can be about many different things. They are often in the first person, end in a question and sometimes are in rhyming couplets such as:

> You need me for sitting but I am not a chair.
> When you are running, I am still there.
> People think I'm soft but I'm hard to find,
> Because wherever you look, I'm always behind.
> What am I?
> The answer is: your bottom.

Teaching idea: Riddles

Ask the children if they know any riddles. The website riddles.com has a huge amount to use as examples and are themed in categories.

Explain to the children that they are going write a riddle about an animal. They need to think about any distinguishing physical features of that animal that they could include, such as feathers, a shell, horns, the colour of the fur, how many legs it has, the eye colour, height, length, etc. They could also consider any other noticeable features such as where it lives, what it eats, its speed, habits, etc.

You could use sentence starters as prompts such as:

> I live in the . . .
> My favourite food is . . .
> On my skin is . . .
> I like to . . .
> What am I?

The children could then add additional information about their animals using their own sentences once the prompts have got them writing. Once completed, the children could read to their partners and guess each other's animals.

After the riddles have been shared, the children could then write a riddle about anything they want. It could be a riddle about another animal or something completely different. In the story, the answers were age, an egg and a name. The children could write about something rather abstract like age, time, space, etc. They might also choose a colour, weather, country, ocean, etc. You could even encourage them to choose something in the classroom. Something they can see might make it easier for them. For example:

I am made of wood but I can also be plastic.
I make things disappear.
I have a fluffy bottom.
You can find me with a pen.
What am I?
Answer: a whiteboard rubber.

10 Whuppity Stoorie (Scottish)

This story is almost identical to 'Rumpelstiltskin', which originated in Germany. However, there are versions of the story from all over Europe. There is 'The Seven Bits of Bacon Rind' from Italy, 'Tom Tit Tot' from England, 'The Girl Who Could Spin Gold from Clay and Long Straw' from Sweden and 'Kinkach Martinko' from Poland. In each story there is name guessing, but the nameless main character varies from fairy to goblin to witch. In all these stories, the hero is always female, apart from the Mongolian story of 'The Use of Magic Language' in which it is a man who has to guess the name. Whatever the origin of these stories, they remain popular to this day.

Whuppity Stoorie

There was once an old woman who lived on a croft named Kittlerumpit with her baby son. The old woman grew carrots, leeks, potatoes and all kinds of vegetables, and kept a large pig called Chops. She worked hard and lived on vegetable soup with the occasional bowl of porridge. The baby's belly was always filled with milk and Chops ate well enough, too. She had to, as she was expecting piglets any day now.

One morning, the old woman woke up to hear a terrible oinking and groaning coming from the pig pen outside of her house. She checked on the baby, then dressed quickly and hurried to the pen. There was Chops on her back with four trotters held up into the air. The pig was grunting and thrashing around. The old woman hurried to the house and got warm water and towels. Perhaps the piglets were arriving!

Chops continued to groan and moan, but no piglets arrived. The old woman realised that she needed a vet, but there were no vets for miles around. She didn't know what to do. She wiped the brow of the suffering pig and spoke to her kindly. She rubbed the sore belly and said prayer after prayer for poor Chops.

By midday, the pig was no better and the old woman was certain that the pig would surely die. The old woman began to cry and wail.

'My sow and her piglets will die! What am I to do? If only there was someone who could help!'

Just then, the garden gate swung open and there was a click-clack, click-clack, click-clack upon the cobblestone path that led through the garden to the house. The old woman was not used to visitors as she lived so far from anyone at all. She looked up and saw a lady wearing a fine gown with laces on the collar and sleeves. She wore a tall top hat and horn-rimmed glasses. The lady was very tall and wore huge black boots. She leaned upon a shiny cane and peered down her nose at the old woman and the pig.

'Whatever is the matter?' snapped the lady. 'I could hear you from the Highlands.'

'My poor pig is dying and her piglets, too! What will I do?' sobbed the old woman.

The lady's eyes flashed and a thin smile curled upon her lips.

'I can help your pig,' she said quietly.

'Really?' gasped the old woman. 'Please do! Please do! I'll give you anything!'

The lady narrowed her eyes.

'Anything?'

'Anything in the world!'

The lady then stepped towards the pig and peered down at her.

'Move aside, then, and let me work,' snapped the lady.

The old woman did as she was told and moved to one side. The lady kneeled down and took out a bottle of black liquid from her dress. She flicked a few drops here and there over Chops and began to mutter under her breath. The old woman could only make out parts of what was being said and it sounded like a great deal of nonsense to her.

> Pitter patter, holy water.
> Spitter spatter, devil's daughter.
> Bitter batter, witch's wand.
> Mitter matter, magic beyond.

Then the lady began to rub the black liquid all over Chops. She rubbed it onto the belly, the legs, trotters, ears, nose and tail. A strong stench filled the air. The pig sneezed a few times and then got to her feet. She was no longer groaning, but rather gave a merry little 'oink' and trotted off around the garden.

The old woman was delighted and clapped her hands with delight. The lady stood as still as a statue and just glared at the old woman.

'Now my fee.'

'Oh, yes!' beamed the old woman. 'Well, as you can see, I have lots of vegetables here. Or perhaps if you would return in a few days, then I could give you a piglet. Chops should give birth any day now. You can have the pick of the litter!'

'I don't want piglets or potatoes,' snapped the lady. 'I want your son.'

The old woman's eyes nearly popped from her head. She opened and closed her mouth a few times.

'That baby, inside your house. I'll take him.'

'Never!' gasped the old woman.

'It's not much to ask. He's surely a burden on you, living here all by yourself. I'll be doing you a favour.'

The old woman began to wail and wring her hands. She paced this way and that.

'You can't take my baby!'

'I can and will,' barked the lady. 'You made a deal. You said that you would give me anything, so I'll return in three days from now and collect the little man.'

'Is there no other way?' cried the old woman.

'Well,' replied the lady sinisterly and, with a smug smile, she added, 'If you guess my name, then you can keep him.'

With that, she turned and walked away along the path with a click-clack, click-clack, click-clack. Then she was through the garden gate and away. The old woman rushed into the house and scooped up her sleeping son. She held him close and sobbed. She cried by day and at night.

The next day, the old woman wouldn't put the baby down. She wailed, cried, wept and sobbed as she clutched on to him. What was she to do? Day turned into night, but she could not sleep. Perhaps she could run away? But where would they go? She had no money and all the food they had grew in her garden.

After a sleepless night, the old woman paced around her house, then the garden and then the house again. Eventually, she decided to go for a walk in the woods nearby. Perhaps it would be there that she might think of what to do. There had to be something the lady would accept instead of her precious baby.

Once in the woods, still holding the baby tightly, the old woman wandered slowly, lost in thought. After a while, she came to a cool, clear river. She set the baby down on the soft grass and took a long drink. Just then, she heard the sound of someone singing. She sat up and looked around. Then she scooped up the baby and followed the sound of the voice.

The old woman also heard the sound of a spinning wheel. This was very curious. Who would spin thread out in the woods? The sound grew louder and seemed to be coming from deep inside the woods. She followed the sound and was led into the gloom. Eventually, the singing was as clear as day. The old woman peered around the trunk of a thick tree and there was the lady. She was sitting on a three-legged stool in front of a spinning wheel, singing and spinning a fine golden thread. The lady sang in a high-pitched voice as she spun:

> Whuppity Stoorie is my name,
> She never knew it when I came.

Then the lady burst into shrill laughter. She cackled until she could no longer spin and tears rolled down her cheeks beneath the horn-rimmed glasses.

'So, that's her name!' gasped the old woman.

Wasting no time, the old woman softly padded away from the woods and back to her home, whispering to her baby with delight.

Both baby and mother slept soundly that night. The next day, the old woman was sitting on a rocking chair in the garden of her house. She cuddled the baby in her arms with a contented smile upon her face.

Just then, the garden gate swung open and with a click-clack, click-clack, click-clack, along came the lady on the cobblestone path. The old woman hid her smile quickly.

'Here I am,' announced the lady. 'Hand over the baby.'

'Oh, no!' cried the old woman. 'Please don't take the baby! Take Chops instead!'

'I don't want your pig!' shrieked the lady. 'Hand over the baby.'

'Take me, then!'

'Why would I want you? You're a useless old woman!' the lady snapped.

'Useless am I, Whuppity Stoorie?'

The old woman smiled at the lady. Her face fell and her mouth hung open.

'I know your name,' the old woman grinned. 'Now be off with you!'

The lady stamped her foot and steam came out of her ears. She turned and ran along the path with a quick click-clack, click-clack, click-clack and never bothered the old woman again.

Chops gave birth to twelve healthy piglets the very next day. The old woman sold eleven of them at the market and made a heap of golden coins. She kept the twelfth piglet and named it Whuppity Stoorie.

Teaching idea: Magic potions

Whuppity Stoorie cured the pig with her potion and magic words. Ask the children to make a list of ingredients for a magic potion. These could be real or imaginary. There could be snake's venom, tree sap, a rotten egg or the juice of a mouldy orange. There could also be dragon's blood, mermaid's tears, a phoenix feather or the scale of a basilisk. For ingredient ideas, take a look at 'The Song of the Witches' in *Macbeth* by William Shakespeare. There could be inspiration from the words of the three witches, such as 'Eye of newt, and toe of frog, Wool of bat, and tongue of dog,' etc. The ingredients could be written like a recipe:

First, pour in _____ .
Next, a pinch of _____ .
Afterwards, add _____ .
Then, mix in _____ .
After that, some _____ .
Finally, _____ .

Once the potion recipe has been written, the children could then write a spell that has to be said for the magic to work. Whuppity Stoorie said:

Pitter patter, holy water.
Spitter spatter, devil's daughter.
Bitter batter, witch's wand.
Mitter matter, magic beyond.

This contains nonsense words and rhyming couplets. This same pattern could be used to help the children write their own spells. In *George's Marvellous Medicine* by Roald Dahl, there is a spell on p. 34 in 'The Cook-up'. There are nonsense words and rhyming couplets that could be used for inspiration. It might be useful to provide children with some rhyming couplets to use as examples, such as:

_____ splash.

_____ crash.

_____ fizz.

_____ whizz.

_____ pop.

_____ plop.

_____ sizzle.

_____ frizzle.

_____ boom.

_____ room.

Then the recipes and spells could be shared and perhaps read as performance poetry.

11 The cow that ate the piper (Scottish)

Some historians say that bagpipes were invented in Ancient Egypt and were brought to Scotland by the Romans. Yet other historians say that bagpipes were brought from Ireland. Either way, the great Highland bagpipe is a musical instrument native to Scotland. Songs like 'Scotland the Brave' and 'The Highland Fling' have made bagpipe music synonymous with Scotland.

In this story, a travelling Highland piper encounters a dead body and the narrative unfolds from there. There are alternate versions from both Scotland and Ireland in which the piper tricks the farmer into believing the cow on the farm is a flesh-eating cow, but this particular Scottish version gives us an interesting twist, which we can use to help the children plan their own narratives in the same style.

The cow that ate the piper

There was once a piper in the Highlands of Scotland. He was a traveller and made nowhere his home. This piper loved his life. He loved playing the most beautiful music and in return people would give him food and shelter for the night.

But his one problem were his boots, which had great holes in them that would let in the rain or the snow or the mud. His feet were so sore that he wished above everything else that he had a new pair of boots.

One winter, the piper was walking over a hill through a swirling, whirling snowstorm. He had under one arm his pipes and under his other he had his pipe repair kit. The storm was so fierce that the piper wrapped a blanket around himself tightly, looking for a place to spend the night. His feet were giving him terrible trouble and once more he wished that he had a new pair of boots. As he made that wish, he suddenly tripped over something sticking out of the snow.

The piper looked at what had made him trip and there he saw a brand new pair of boots – boots made of a soft brown leather and with a fur lining poking out of the top. The piper looked around and when he saw no one coming to claim the boots, he bent down and tried to pull them out of the snow. He pulled and dragged and heaved out of the snow – a dead body. A dead body frozen stiff. A dead body still wearing the boots.

The piper decided that this dead man wouldn't need these boots any more, so he undid the laces and tried to get them off, but they were frozen solid to the man's feet. Then the piper had an idea. He unwrapped his pipe repair kit and he took out a long, thin saw.

The piper held onto the man's leg, rested the saw just above the foot and began to saw and hack, saw and hack, saw and hack, until he came to the bone. Then it was really hard going! Saw and hack, saw and hack, saw and hack. Eventually, one foot came off. So he started on the other leg. Saw and hack, saw and hack, saw and hack, until the other came off, too.

Finally, the piper threw the boots, with the feet still inside, over his shoulder. Holding them by the laces, he gathered his pipes and his repair kit, then set off to find shelter and perhaps even somewhere to defrost his new boots.

After a while, the piper came to an old farmhouse. He put the frozen boots down near a barn, as there's nothing stranger than knocking on someone's door with a pair of feet in your hands! The piper knocked at the door and an old woman answered.

'Who are you and what do you want?' she croaked.

'I'm a piper,' he explained. 'I was hoping that I could perhaps have some food and shelter for the night and in return I'll play my pipes.'

'Oooh!' squealed the old woman. 'We like a bit of pipe music, but we haven't much room in the house. You'll have to sleep in the barn over there with the cow. Come in, come in!'

The farmer was sitting by the fire and said, 'Who's this, then, wife?'

'He's a piper, he going to play us some music!'

And that's exactly what he did. The piper played all night long and the farmer and his wife had a fantastic night; they clapped and sang and danced. The piper had a grand night, too; he had three bowls of broth and many glasses of whisky. Then, at the end of the night, the piper bid the farmer and his wife a good evening and set off to sleep in the barn. He collected the frozen feet on his way in. The piper noticed the cow sleeping on the straw. He went over and patted the cow just to be polite, and, as he did so, he couldn't help noticing how warm the cow felt.

'This could be an excellent place to defrost my feet!' he said to himself.

So, the piper pushed the frozen boots under the cow, lay down on the straw and fell fast asleep.

In the morning, his first thought was his aching and sore feet. He remembered his boots under the cow and went over to see if they had defrosted. He pulled the boots out from under the cow and as he did so, the cow got to her feet. Sure enough, there was a pool of blood; the feet had defrosted. So, the piper undid the laces and with a *slurghpt!* he pulled out one foot. Then with a *slurghpt!* he pulled out the other foot.

The piper took off his old boots, slipped on the new ones and they felt glorious. He felt like doing a dance and a jig right there in the middle of the barn. But when he saw the old, mouldy feet and the worn, broken boots, he wondered what he should do with them. As the piper stood there, staring at them he had an idea; he pushed the old, mouldy feet into the worn, broken boots.

Now, the piper had drunk so much the night before that he needed to pee, but he didn't want to wake the farmer and his wife, so went round the back of the barn for his early morning pee.

Meanwhile, the farmer and his wife had woken up. The farmer's wife said, 'That piper last night was brilliant! I'm going to make him his breakfast.'

She made three bowls of porridge and three mugs of tea. Then she went outside to the barn and knocked at the door. The door swung open and there she saw a pool of blood and the piper's old boots with two stumps sticking out of them – and she also saw the cow standing above the boots chewing away.

'*Aaarrrggghhh*!' she screamed. 'The cow's eaten the piper!'

She ran to get her husband and dragged him into the barn. 'The cow's eaten the piper!' she kept saying.

The farmer and his wife looked into the barn. There the farmer saw the blood and the boots and the cow.

'*Aaarrrggghhh*!' they both screamed as they ran off never to be seen again.

Now the piper heard the scream, so he came back around the barn looked inside. When he couldn't see the farmer and his wife, the piper went to the house. He knocked at the kitchen door and the door swung open. The piper saw the three mugs and tea and the three bowls of porridge.

'I must be getting my breakfast, too!' he said to himself.

He went inside, sat down, drank the tea and ate the porridge. The piper then waited for the farmer and his wife to come home, but they didn't. So he decided to do a few jobs on the farm to look after the place until they came home.

That night, he slept on the kitchen floor and in the morning made himself some breakfast before working on the farm.

Two nights became three. Three nights became four. Four nights became a week. A week became two weeks. Two weeks became a month. A month became three months. The piper discovered that he loved living and working on the farm. There was to be no more travelling as this was the life for him. He would stay right there until the farmer and his wife came home.

One night, when the piper was sitting with his feet up by the fire – wearing his new boots, of course – there came a knock . . . knock . . . knock at the door.

The piper answered it and there standing in the doorway was a man – a very *short* man – a short man with *no feet*!

'I've come for my feet,' he said grimly.

'*Aaarrrggghhh*!' screamed the piper, as he ran off and was never seen again.

But what has been seen again, walking around the Highlands of Scotland, is a very short man with no feet. And, if you see him, then stay away because he might be after yours!

Teaching idea: Third person and past tense

Ask the children what they think the short man with no feet might look like. Ask them to draw portraits of this ghostly figure. They might include frozen features from the snow, gaping eye-sockets or rotting flesh. It might resemble a zombie or have skeletal features. Then the children could label the key features of their portrait. Now they would have a ghostly character and could begin to plan a narrative ghost story around this character.

The story of the piper is written in the third person and is in the past tense. The children could also plan their stories to be in the third person and past tense, too. They should choose a main character which could be a man, woman, boy or girl. This character needs a reason to be travelling around the Highlands of Scotland. Perhaps they could be a musician or storyteller travelling from place to place. They might even just be walking from one place to another, but a reason needs to be given so that the narrative makes sense.

The setting for the story ended up being a farm late at night. The children need to choose a night-time setting for their story. I'd recommend that their setting should be abandoned in order to create a spooky setting description. They could choose any setting they like, such as a graveyard, forest, mineshaft, beach, library, mansion, doctor's surgery, museum, prison or cave.

However, their character visiting an abandoned setting late at night doesn't make sense unless a reason why is added. In the story, the piper knocks at the door of the farmhouse in order to ask if he can stay the night. The children need to include a reason why their character has arrived at their chosen setting. Here are some possible reasons:

- the character is lost;

- they were dared to go there;

- they are looking for a lost family member or pet;

- their dog got off the lead;

- the character heard there might be treasure or money;

- they are looking for adventure;

- they heard someone calling for help;

- they were there earlier in the day and lost something valuable.

Once the children have explained why their character is in the setting, they could include some descriptions of the setting. If it is abandoned, they could describe features such as rotting wood, spiders' webs, dust-covered surfaces, broken furniture, etc.

The weather could also feature, making the place seem even spookier, such as a ghostly fog, dark clouds covering the moon, thunder rumbling overhead or a howling wind.

The children could introduce the ghost character which they designed earlier. This might lead to a cliff-hanger ending. In the story, the piper screamed and was never seen again. The children could use this or adapt it to make the story their own. They might write something like:

- The ghost got closer and closer. The girl screamed. It was the last thing she ever saw.

- The man turned to run away, but the dead fingers found warm flesh.

- The ghost smiled a leering grin and rasped, 'You'll never leave this place.'

- She ran and ran. She would never go back to that place.

- The ghost sadly whispered, 'Don't leave me.'

- The man screamed in terror but the ghost smiled in a friendly way. Was there nothing to fear?

- Then the ghost disappeared into the swirling fog. The mist cleared and she was all alone.

- She shone her torch at the ghost and it faded away into nothing.

- He ran home, but when he got there the ghost was waiting for him.

- She turned away from the ghost, but there were many more ghostly figures behind her.

12 Jack the Giant Killer (English)

Jack's second adventure is a bloodthirsty adventure involving the gory deaths of many giants at the boy's hands. Jack is known as originating from Cornwall, but his origins go way back further than this. The first printing of the story was in 1711, but it would have been told orally well before then during Celtic times, and the story likely predates even that. For example, when Jack tricks Thunderdell the giant, it seems to be based on a myth where Thor tricks Skrymir the giant. Therefore, the story is likely to be of Norse origin.

Jack the Giant Killer

Once upon a time, I travelled to a village and liked it there so much that I decided to stay. There was one problem with this village, though – a problem that the villagers had not told me about until *after* I had parted with several golden coins to rent a house. It was a giant – a giant named Cormoran.

Cormoran would come into the village on a night and eat anybody he could find. If there was nobody about, then he would steal sheep or cows or pigs from any nearby farm. Now, I'd dealt with a giant before, so I sat and thought of a plan as to how I could teach this big fellow a lesson. After a while, I went off with a shovel and a sword.

I arrived at the bottom of Cormoran's mountain and set to work. I dug a great hole in the ground, then covered this with leaves and sticks and branches. Just before nightfall, I called up to Cormoran:

'Oi! Wake up!'

'*Who's that, then?*' he bellowed down to me.

'It's me, Jack!' I replied. 'Come down here. We need to set a few things straight!'

'*You'll be going straight down my throat*!' he shouted and sprinted down the mountain to gobble me up.

With a thud, Cormoran landed straight in the hole I'd dug. The hole was deep but narrow, so he had his arms stuck securely against his body and was unable to climb out.

'*Get me out of here*!' the giant boomed.

'Not until you promise never to eat people or steal livestock again,' I demanded.

'*Never!*' came his reply.

So, I lopped off Cormoran's head with my sword. I then dragged his great body out of the hole and took off his boots and put them on. Wearing Cormoran's boots, I strode back into the village. The boots were so big that they came right up to my waist!

'Come out, everyone! Cormoran is dead!' I announced to the fearful village.

Cautiously, people stepped out of their houses and stood agog. The mayor of the village was delighted and gave me a golden sash to wear around my body. It said: 'Giant Killer'.

After a few days celebrating, I left that village in search of more adventure. In no time at all I came across a giant's castle among some hills and I decided to take a look. As soon as I walked up to the drawbridge, it came down with a thud. I only just managed to leap to safety or I would have been crushed.

A huge giant called Blunderbore looked at me and laughed:

'Giant Killer, eh? We'll soon see how many giants you can kill if you're locked in a prison cell! Ha! Ha! Ha!'

Blunderbore scooped me up and took me to his dungeon. He then threw me into a prison cell and locked the door. The problem with giant prisons is that they don't really keep folks like you and me locked up very well. I was able to slip between the great metal bars without even having to breathe in. Then I sneaked my way around the castle and discovered it was deserted. From outside the castle I could hear Blunderbore talking to another giant.

'I've got the little pipsqueak locked up in my dungeon! Let's go back and share him for our supper!' said Blunderbore.

'Yeah! We'll teach him to wear the words "Giant Killer"!' said his brother Rebecks.

I raced up to the battlements and, using my sword, I sliced the ropes that held the drawbridge. The drawbridge landed with a bang right onto the heads of the two giants. While they were stunned and reeling, I tied two great loops into the drawbridge ropes and whirled them both over my head, one in each hand. I then threw the ropes like lassos over their heads. I pulled the ropes as hard as I could so that the giants' necks were choked. Their eyes nearly popped from their heads and they slumped dead in front of the castle. I was really getting the hang of this giant killing!

Well, off I went seeking more adventure. A little later, I was walking through a forest when I came across a most peculiar sight. A two-headed giant called Thunderdell was sitting on a log devouring a dead deer. He looked at me for a moment, stared for a long time at my golden sash, and then invited me to his house for dinner and a bed for the night. I cheerfully accepted and allowed him to scoop me up with his hand and carry me home. I had a huge dinner of roast beef, potatoes and vegetables. I then climbed into a gigantic bed in Thunderdell's spare room and was drifting off to sleep when I heard the two-headed giant talking to himself.

'He'll be asleep by now, then we can grab our club and beat him to death while he sleeps!'

'Brilliant plan!'

Thunderdell was trying to whisper these words, but the problem with giants is that they can't whisper very well, so I heard every word. I then leapt from the bed and grabbed some logs that were stacked up by the fire. I made a 'Jack-shaped' model of myself out of the logs in the bed and covered it up with the blankets. I was hiding under the bed when the two-headed giant arrived carrying his club. He bashed and beat and banged at the bed before going off to his own bed, chuckling all the way.

In the morning, I strode downstairs to the kitchen where Thunderdell was sitting, eating a massive bowl of porridge.

'Morning!' I smiled.

'*Eh?*' one of the heads said.

'*How come you're not dead?*' asked the other. '*Couldn't you feel anything hitting your body last night?*'

'Well, I could feel moths tickling me, but that was all!' I replied.

Thunderdell giant looked stunned and scared.

'Can I have a big bowl of porridge, same as you, please?' I asked.

The two-headed giant nodded hurriedly and rushed off to make me my breakfast. I grabbed hold of a sack that was lying on the floor and stuffed it under my jacket. When Thunderdell placed the porridge respectfully in front of me, I pretended to eat it, but all the while I was spooning it into the sack under my jacket.

When the bowl was empty, I said, 'Can I have another, please?'

'*Aren't you full up yet?*' asked Thunderdell.

'Oh, when I get full up, I simply do this!'

I plunged my sword into my jacket and cut open the sack. The porridge spilt all over the floor.

'There, now I'm hungry again. Another, please!' I grinned.

'*I've never seen that before!*' one giant head exclaimed. '*I want to try that!*'

Thunderdell took my sword and plunged it into his own belly. He instantly fell down dead on the floor. I cleaned my sword and swaggered out of there.

A few days later, I came to the foothills of a mountain where an old man was sitting.

'Don't go up there!' he warned me. 'There is terrible danger.'

'I'm Jack the Giant Killer!' I announced. 'Nothing scares me!'

'Well, in that case let me offer you a gift!' said the old man and he handed me a cloak. 'This is an invisibility cloak. When you wear it, you're invisible!'

'Thanks a lot! Very handy,' I replied.

With the cloak in one hand and my sword in the other, I set off up the mountain. Half-way up, I saw two dragons guarding a large set of iron gates. I pulled the invisibility cloak over my head and sneaked my way past them.

At the top, I saw the biggest giant I had ever seen in my life. He was called Galligantus and was bent down talking to an evil-looking wizard. I held my sword out in front of me and approached them. Galligantus stood to his full height and looked at the 'floating' sword getting closer. The wizard looked utterly baffled. Galligantus bent right down on his knees to get a closer look and as he did, I swung the sword and chopped off his head.

When the wizard saw a 'floating' sword beat his giant, he screamed and ran off down the mountain. I saw him take flight, standing on the backs of the two dragons and disappear into the dark clouds above. I flung the invisibility cloak off and explored the top of the mountain.

There was a large castle and gardens. In the gardens were statues of all kinds of animals. In the centre of the garden was a large silver trumpet hanging from a mighty oak tree. I took the trumpet and blew as hard as I could. Suddenly the statues began to move.

There was a great crunching sound as the stone animals came to life, shed their stone skin, shed their animal skin and became human. One of the statues became a living deer and then the most beautiful girl I had ever seen.

'Thank you for saving us!' she said as she rushed forward, threw her arms around me and showered me with kisses. 'My name is Jill.'

'I'm Jack,' I beamed back.

Just then, the old man arrived.

'Father!' beamed Jill. 'This young man has saved us.'

'I know,' he smiled back. 'We've met.'

I stayed in that castle up in the mountains for many years, living happily with the old man and his daughter, Jill. Was it happily ever after? Well, you know me, there were more adventures to be had for Jack the Giant Killer.

About this story

Jack's story is full of giants and could give the children ideas to design their own giant characters. They could have giants with three heads, one eye, horns, be covered in fur, or have many arms and legs. The giant in the story of Jack and the Beanstalk said, 'Fee-fi-fo-fum'.

Teaching idea: Designing giants

Younger children could replace the letter 'f' with a different consonant so that the nonsense words begin with a different sound, such as 'Mee-mi-mo-mum', 'Pee-pi-po-pum' or 'Bee-bi-bo-bum'.

Older children could extend what the giants say by writing their own rhyme. For example:

> Fee-fi-fo-fum,
> I smell the blood of an Englishman.
> Be he alive or be he dead,
> I'll grind his bones to make my bread!

could become

> Nee-ni-no-num,
> I smell the socks of a stinky son.
> Be he here or be he there,
> I'll feed him to my bear.

or

> See-si-so-sum,
> I hear the shout of an angry chum.
> Be she quiet or be she loud,
> I'll throw her up into a cloud.

Once the children have their giant character and the things they say, they could then think about how Jack would defeat each one. He uses traps to kill Cormoran, Blunderbore and Rebecks. He uses trickery to beat Thunderdell. A magic object is used against Galligantus. The children could think about traps, tricks and magic items for their own Jack story, too. The traps could involve digging holes or ropes to bind, as in the story, but the children could also add their own ideas such as using bait, cages, nets or secret doors. The tricks might involve using decoys, glue, food or drink. Magic items could be something to turn Jack invisible, but could also be something that makes him fly, run super-fast, breathe underwater or talk to animals.

Once the children have their ideas, then they could write action scenes to show how Jack defeats the giants. The children should make sure that they are adding enough detail. Instead of writing:

Jack dropped a cage on the giant and trapped him

it could be expanded into something like:

Jack chopped down ten trees and built a wooden cage with them. The giant was looking for Jack. He was hiding in a tall tree. The giant walked underneath the tree. Jack dropped the cage and it landed on him. He screamed angrily and wanted to be let out.

In that example, the writing was structured so that Jack did something and the giant did something else. This was repeated three times. The children could follow that same narrative pattern:

First, Jack . . .
After that, the giant . . .
Next, Jack . . .
Then, the giant . . .
Afterwards, Jack . . .
Finally, the giant . . .

This could be repeated for each different giant with a different plan for Jack. The children could then be encouraged to select different sentence openers other than just using time conjunctions.

13 The Draiglin Hogney (Scottish)

Perhaps the best known version of the story comes from The Scottish Fairy Book *written by Elizabeth Wilson Grierson in 1910. In it, the Draiglin Hogney is a giant with a bushy beard. The word 'draiglin' is an old Scottish word for unkept and the word 'hogney' most likely means a demon of some sort. Whether giant or demon, he is always described as having messy hair, long tusks and glowing eyes. Celtic stories often have these monstrous characters such as the Wulver, a creature similar to a werewolf, the Bean Nighe, which is a banshee, or Kelpies, which are like sea demons. Often these characters have magical weapons like the staff in this story.*

The Draiglin Hogney

There was once a poor old couple who lived in the Lowlands with their two sons and one daughter. They grew their own food and lived off the land as best they could. They were all keen hunters and kept horses for chasing deer, dogs for chasing foxes and hawks for chasing rabbits.

One day, the eldest son decided to ride off and seek his fortune in the Highlands. He took with him his horse, his hound and his hawk. As he rode high up in the hills, he came to a deep and dark forest. The forest was still and quiet, and not even a single ray of sunshine could be seen under the vast leaves of the trees. The forest was utterly silent with not a single bird song. The horse pinned back its ears as if trying to hear anything at all, the hound walked with its tail between its legs and the hawk flew close to the eldest son.

Eventually, the eldest son came to a clearing where a huge castle stood. The windows glittered with precious stones and the door was made from the purest gold. The eldest son slipped down from his saddle and led the horse towards the door. The horse pulled and whinnied in fright, but the eldest son forcefully dragged the poor horse onwards. The door then opened by itself, revealing a long corridor with a marble floor. The horse's hooves sounded out loudly on the marble as they walked along it.

They finally arrived in a huge banqueting hall. There was a vast table lined with silver plates. Each plate was covered in roasted meats, delicious vegetables and every cake you could imagine. There were great goblets of rich wine.

There was food for the horse, hound and hawk, too: hay for the horse and meat for the hound and hawk. They all sat down and began to feast.

When their bellies were bursting, the eldest son saw that it was very late. A tall grandfather clock in the corner of the room began to chime out with twelve loud rings. It was midnight and, on the last chime, the door was flung open and in walked a towering man.

'I am the Draiglin Hogney,' the man boomed. 'This is my castle.'

The eldest son gasped as the Draiglin Hogney stepped into the candlelight. He had huge, pointed ears and a massive bulbous nose. Two long tusks, like a walrus, stuck out from below a bushy moustache. His hair and beard were thick and red. His clawed feet tapped over the marble floor. One of his clawed hands held a walking stick carved into a snake head at the top. The Draiglin Hogney had eyes of flame. They glowed orange and wide.

'Thank you for supper,' the boy called, gulping slightly. 'That was very kind of you.'

The Draiglin Hogney smiled, which made drool run down his two tusk-like teeth. He sat down in a leather armchair by the fire.

'Come and join me, boy. But leave the beasts where they are.'

There was another armchair by the fire and the Draiglin Hogney pointed at it.

'Aye, all right.'

'But we don't want your beasts wandering over to us now, do we? Your horse might kick me, your dog might bite me and your hawk might scratch me. I'm a sensitive soul, you see.'

'They won't . . . '

The boy suddenly stopped speaking as the Draiglin Hogney pulled out three red hairs from his beard.

'Tie these around their collars. That will keep the beasts away.'

Well, the boy didn't want to be rude, so he took the three hairs, then tied one to the horse's bridle, one to the dog's collar and one to the hawk's jess.

'That's better,' grinned the Draiglin Hogney and more drool escaped his mouth. 'Now you're mine!'

He stood up and pointed the snake head at the eldest son. The eyes began to glow green. The horse, hound and hawk strained to help their master, but the three hairs held them like chains.

Back in the Lowlands, the parents, brother and sister of the eldest son had searched and searched for him, but days had passed and he had not returned home. The youngest son decided he would take his horse, hound and hawk to find his brother.

He, too, found the forest, then the castle and went inside.

'Hello?' he called along the corridor that led to the banqueting hall. 'Is there anyone there? Brother?'

The boy had been searching all day, so when he saw that the food was making the table sag, he was only too happy to sit and eat. The horse, hound and hawk were also delighted after a such a long journey.

When the clock struck midnight, in came the Draiglin Hogney who introduced himself and sat down by the fire. The boy firmly believed that you shouldn't judge people by how they look, so even if the Draiglin Hognery had fangs down to his chest and drool that dripped every time he smiled, the boy still obliged in taking the hairs and tying up his animals. The horse whinnied, the dog snarled and the hawk screeched in protest.

'Don't be silly!' cried the youngest brother. 'They're only hairs!'

But when the Draiglin Hogney turned his snake head walking-stick on to the boy, he gasped in horror. The green eyes of the snake glowed.

'I already have your brother as my slave!' laughed the Draiglin Hogney. 'Now I have you!'

The animals screamed with rage, but they were helpless.

Back in the Lowlands, the parents and sister of the two brothers were out of their minds with worry. The daughter decided that she would find her brother. She took her horse, hound and hawk and set off. Her parents waved her off with tears in their eyes.

When she arrived at the forest, her first thought was to ride around it as it looked a dangerous place. But she knew her brothers' thirst for adventure and guessed that they had probably gone inside.

She came to the palace and as soon as she saw the precious stones and gold, she knew at once that her brothers would be trapped inside, lured by the treasure. She shook her head and went in.

Although she and her animals were very hungry, they didn't eat a single crumb of food. She decided that the whole place was very much a trap, so sat down by the fire to wait to see what would happen next.

Sure enough, when the twelve chimes were struck, the Draiglin Hogney came inside and sat down in the chair next to the daughter.

'Take those animals away, let them eat.'

'They're fine, thanks.'

'Well, the horse might kick me, the dog might bite me and the hawk might scratch me.'

The Draiglin Hogney pulled free three red hairs and offered them to the girl.

'Tie them up with these.'

The daughter could smell the magic on the hairs and flicked them onto the fire before pretending to tie up the horse, hound and hawk.

'All done. Is that better?' asked the girl.

'Aye, it is!' grinned the Draiglin Hogney. 'I already have your brothers and now you'll be my slave too!'

He turned his snake head walking-stick towards the girl. She knew this to be a magic staff and leapt up from the chair. At that moment the hawk scratched at the flaming eyes of the

Draiglin Hogney, the horse kicked him onto the fire and the dog snatched the stick away. He roared in pain and anger, but then the girl took the stick from the dog. She turned the snake head towards the Draiglin Hogney and he dissolved into the fire.

'Let us find my brothers!' the girl said to her animals.

They searched that castle from top to bottom and found great chests filled with emeralds, diamonds, rubies, pearls, sapphires and many golden coins. But in the cellar, the two brothers were chained up along with countless other young men. The daughter used the magic staff to break the chains and free them all.

'I wonder what else this staff can do?' she cried. 'I'm going to have great fun finding out!'

The daughter shared the treasure equally between them all and everyone went home wealthy and happy. Back in the Lowlands, the family was reunited and lived happily for the rest of their days.

Teaching idea: The demon

The Draiglin Hogney's face, feet and hands are described in the story, but not its body. Ask the children to draw full body portraits of the demon. Then reread the physical description of the demon to check if the children remembered the features of the nose, teeth, beard, moustache, feet, hands and eyes. Ask the children to label their portraits with noun phrases. They could use adjectives from the story, but could also upgrade these with their own ideas. So the description could then be rewritten using the extra adjectives. The original description:

> He had huge, pointed ears and a massive bulbous nose. Two long tusks, like a walrus, stuck out from below a bushy moustache. His hair and beard were thick and red. His clawed feet tapped over the marble floor. One of his clawed hands held a walking stick carved into a snake head at the top. The Draiglin Hogney had eyes of flame. They glowed orange and wide.

could become:

> He had huge, long, pointed and sharp ears. His nose was massive, bulbous, warty and round. Two long, sharp, deadly tusks, like a walrus, stuck out from below a messy, wild and bushy moustache. His hair and beard were thick, tangled and bright red. His clawed feet were curved, deadly and loud as they tapped over the marble floor. One of his savage and vicious clawed hands held an inky black walking-stick with a sinister snake head carved at the top. The Draiglin Hogney had gigantic, wide eyes of fiery flames. They glowed bright orange and wide.

Once this description has been written, the children could then label the rest of the demon with noun phrases and turn these into a descriptive paragraph. They could include descriptions of the arms, legs and body. They could also add wings, a tail, horns and any other features they can imagine.

The children could then go on to design their own demon character and use the same descriptive techniques to describe this new demon. You could give the children some adjectives to use as a model or also to 'magpie' from. These could be grouped according to the body part of the character, such as:

Face: creased, lipless, hollow, ghoulish, deadly, vicious, wide, expressionless.

Hands/arms: long, twisted, veiny, bony, skinny, twig-like, distorted, sharp.

Legs/feet: jagged, dagger-like, curled, warty, webbed, lumpy, armoured, tough.

Body: massive, vast, towering, veiny, ancient, immense, hairy, powerful.

The Draiglin Hogney had a magical staff. The new demon character could have different magical objects such as potions, jewellery, wands, books, scrolls, a dagger, a crystal ball, etc. The staff in the story makes people slaves. Ask the children what their demon character uses each object for. Perhaps the demon could have a death potion that summons a skeleton army, an eyeball necklace that can see into the future or a unicorn shoe that can control magical animals.

Once all the information has been gathered and the ideas have been shared, the children could then write their own demon descriptions.

14 The white dragon and the red dragon (Welsh)

This story is about King Vortigern, a fifth-century warlord who took refuge in Wales to escape the invading Anglo-Saxons. The Welsh flag is named 'Y Ddraig Goch', which means 'the red dragon'. In 1485, Henry VII displayed a red dragon flag at the Battle of Bosworth where Richard III was defeated. It is likely that the Welsh flag is based on this flag, but its origins go much further back in history. Some historians believe that it goes back to Roman cavalry standards. Other historians believe that it originated in medieval times. Whatever the origin, it is perhaps the most striking flag in the world and this story attempts to explain why the red dragon is associated with Wales.

The white dragon and the red dragon

King Vortigern had travelled long and far, but at last he had found the perfect place. He had escaped Anglo-Saxon invaders at every turn and now the Celtic king smiled. He stopped his horse on the shore of the lake Llyn Dinas and gazed up at the mountain. This was covered in a dense woodland which would be perfect for the timber he would need. The River Glaslyn coiled its way around the base of the mountain. Vast rocks lined the river, too. So there was a water source, a good supply of wood and stone. It was also at an excellent vantage point in case of any invaders. Vortigern smiled wider – perfection.

The king turned to his army that had assembled behind him. The Celtic warriors looked at the leader with anticipation.

'Here,' Vortigern announced. 'We will camp here and begin construction in the morning.'

There were carpenters, stone masons and builders assembled in his army, too. A stronghold would first be built and then a mountain fort. This fortress would eventually be a castle – the finest castle this land had ever seen. They would settle here in this beautiful place and all would be well.

The camp was set up beside the lake. Fires were lit and tents built. Vortigern knew that a fortress could not be built in a few days. They needed time.

Each day, the hunters went off into the woods to catch deer, boar and rabbits. Others caught fish and ducks by the river. Fruit and berries were gathered, too. Water was collected from the river. Feeding an army took a lot of organising, but Vortigern was a born leader. He organised the supplies effortlessly. He also worked with the designers of the mountain fort. Woodcutters worked tirelessly and stone masons carved endlessly.

At the end of the day, Vortigern's army travelled back to the camp exhausted, but they had worked hard and made good progress. The royal masons had laid the foundations and there was a feast to be had.

King Vortigern drank deeply from a wooden cup and nodded with approval. All was going to plan. The mountain fort would be ready in mere weeks. He slept soundly in his tent that night beneath animal furs and dreamt of his castle to come.

In the morning, the camp was bustling with activity. Each person knew their role and went about their jobs with an intense efficiency. They were like an army of ants with each person fulfilling their own role perfectly. But when the king and his masons arrived at the building site on the mountain, they all gasped. The foundations had been destroyed. How could this be? There were lookouts in the camp awake all night. It would take a small army to break down stone foundations and none had been heard.

The repairs were made, but these took all day. King Vortigern decided that more lookouts were needed and posted these at the building site on the top of the mountain. They were given wooden torches to light to use in a signal in case they needed any help. This would act as a call for reinforcements if any army, small or large, was to appear.

The next morning, the foundations had been destroyed again. The lookouts insisted that no single person had been there. They had been awake all night and heard no sounds besides the hoot of an owl and the cry of a fox.

So, the repairs were made again and the next morning the same thing happened. Morning after morning it went on. The army worked relentlessly but to no avail.

In the end, King Vortigern decided to seek the advice of a druid. These wise sages would consult the gods and tell him what to do.

A local druid was found and advised the king to find a child born of a mother from this world and a father from the 'other world' – that is, a half-human and half-fairy child. But where could such a child be found?

King Vortigern sent out a group of soldiers to search the land for this child. The group was gone for seven days and seven nights. During this time, the same thing kept happening with the foundations of the mountain fort; they were destroyed by morning.

Eventually, when the group returned, they had with them a child and his mother. He was found near Carmarthen and his mother would only agree to let him go if she could accompany him. Also, she was rewarded with silver for her time and trouble.

'Come here, child,' said King Vortigern. 'You won't be harmed. I need your help!'

The child, around four or five years old, slipped down from his mother's embrace and walked boldly forward to the king.

'Don't be afraid. I only want to ask you a question, that is all.'

The child smiled and said, 'I'm not afraid. Ask your question.'

Impressed, the king kneeled down to the boy.

'Why can't I build upon the mountain up there?'

The child looked up at the mountain. He turned his head slightly and narrowed his eyes. After a few moments he nodded to himself and turned back to the king on one knee.

'There is a lake within the mountain. Your foundations soak up the water and cannot stand strong.'

'Then we shall drain the lake!' said the king.

'Be warned,' continued the child. 'Two dragons sleep in the lake. If you drain it, then you will wake them up.'

The boy then turned away and walked towards his mother.

'What's your name?' asked King Vortigern.

'I am named Myrrdin Emrys,' replied the boy.

His mother scooped him up and turned her horse to ride away.

'But some call me Merlin,' the boy added, before they rode off.

The king watched them go, then nodded to his masons.

'We shall drain the lake. Start immediately.'

'What of the dragons?' asked one mason.

'No such thing!' laughed the king. 'Fairy tales and nothing more.'

So the mountain was tapped and the lake was drained. But no sooner had the water reached the river and lake below than a great rumbling sound could be heard from within the mountain.

The camp watched as one. The mountain-top suddenly burst open and a huge red claw emerged. It gripped the rocky surface of the mountain and tore the top right off. It was an explosion of might and power. A red dragon with vast wings reared up onto its back legs and roared. The camp was frozen with fear. King Vortigern's eyes were wide and his mouth gaped open.

Just then, a white clawed hand appeared and yellow slitted eyes peered from the gap in the mountain. A white dragon slithered through the opening and coiled its way around the mountain-top. The red dragon hadn't yet noticed it. This dragon was looking down at the humans that had woken it up, but it didn't look with anger. Rather, it was looking as though it was making up its mind about them. It stood above the white dragon which began to pad slowly around the mountain. It gave furtive looks up at the red dragon and entered the dense woodland that covered the mountain.

But the red dragon turned and saw the serpent tail of the white dragon flick and twitch before disappearing between the trees. The red dragon lunged forward and grabbed the scaly tail of the white dragon. It was pulled backwards and hissed with rage. It turned and flapped its wings, sending trees falling in all directions. Then it flicked its tail rapidly over and over again until it broke free of the red dragon's grip.

The two dragons turned and glared at each other. They circled the mountain with eyes locked. The red dragon snarled and the white dragon hissed. Then they both attacked at the same time. Their bodies slammed into one another. Tails whipped, teeth snapped and claws scratched. Armour-plated scales offered protection, but the attacks were relentless.

The camp below was transfixed by the terrible scene. They watched with horror as the battle raged on. The red dragon had the white dragon pinned to the ground, but it scratched at the red wings, trying to shred them. With a sudden snap, the red dragon closed its jaws upon the white dragon's neck. It howled with pain and anger. Then, with a mighty heave, it pushed the red dragon backwards. The white dragon knew it was beaten. It could not stand up to the might and power of its opponent. It squatted briefly, then leapt into the air. Its wings scooped up air and flapped into the sky. The red dragon did not pursue it. It had chased the white dragon away and that was enough.

It turned back to the camp at the bottom of the mountain. With narrow eyes it stared at the terrified humans gathered below. Then the gaze softened. The harsh expression from battle was replaced once more with a compassionate look. It stared at King Vortigern, then nodded once. The king smiled. It seemed to him that the dragon was somehow giving its permission to build upon the mountain.

The dragon turned and climbed back into the hole on the mountain. The head went first and the spiky tail seemed to wave farewell as it disappeared. The king had a huge smile. He turned to the others from his horse.

'The dragon has given us its blessing,' he announced. 'The foundations will not fall this time.'

A great cheer went up and the building work began immediately. The mountain fort was soon constructed and was eventually built into a castle. This castle was named Dinas Emrys, so called in honour of the boy who had warned the king about the dragons.

You can visit the ruins of Dinas Emrys Castle on the mountain that holds a sleeping dragon – a dragon that is shown on the Welsh flag to this day. This is to honour the dragon that gave a king permission to build on its mountain.

About this story

In 1945 the site of Dinas Emrys was excavated by archaeologists. They did, indeed, discover a lake and the ruins of a mountain-top fortress that dates back to King Vortigern's time. They also discovered that the walls of the mountain fort showed signs of having been rebuilt several times, so perhaps this story is true!

Most people, however, think of this story as a metaphor. The red dragon is meant to symbolise King Vortigern's army and the white dragon is meant to represent the Saxon invaders. The Anglo-Saxon kingdom of Northumbria had a red flag with a white dragon on it. When King Vortigern successfully repelled the Saxon invaders, this story evolved from that battle.

Teaching idea: Metaphors

Define what a metaphor is to your class after you have read the story. The *Oxford English Dictionary* defines it as: 'A figure of speech in which a word or phrase is applied to an object or action to which it is not literally applicable.' So, the Anglo-Saxons were not literally dragons, but can be described figurately as a white dragon, just as King Vortigern was not literally a dragon but figuratively can be described as a red dragon.

In the story, the two dragons are rivals. Ask the children to choose two rivals – for example, from a game such as *Minecraft*, football teams, animals, fairy tale or fantasy characters, etc. In *Minecraft*, for example, the rivals could be a creeper vs. a zombie. Football teams could be Sunderland vs. Newcastle. Animals could be a lion vs. a hyena. Fairy-tale characters could be a unicorn vs. an ogre. Fantasy characters could be a wizard vs. a witch, etc.

The children could then choose which is the good character and which is the bad one. The children could then write metaphor descriptions of each character. They could use the weather, a vehicle, a setting, a smell, a taste, etc. So, if they were to choose a good creeper vs. a bad zombie, they might write:

> The creeper is the sunshine, bright and cheerful. It is a rollercoaster of excitement travelling at impossibly fun speed. It is a day out at the beach with your family. It is the smell of candy floss from the fair. It is the sweetest taste of success.

> But the zombie is a thunderstorm, dark and brooding. It is a broken-down car on a busy road. It is a prison cell of doom. It is the stench of death. It is the taste of blood.

The children could go on to describe a race, penalty shootout, wrestling match or any kind of competition between the two characters where the good character succeeds and the bad character is chased away or beaten. Metaphor descriptions could be used throughout once the children have practised this method of figurative description.

15 Jack and the fish (English)

Unlike 'Jack and the Beanstalk' and 'Jack the Giant Killer', the character of Jack in this story is lazy. In many Jack stories he is not only lazy but foolish too, yet always uses his wits and charm to be victorious in the end. We have all done foolish things and perhaps been lazy at certain times in our lives and these stories were meant to entertain us by hearing about someone else being the foolish one. They were told to make us smile as Lazy Jack wins the day despite the many flaws in his character.

Jack and the fish

Once upon a time, when I was living up that mountain with my wife, Jill, I had grown lazy – very lazy. I was known as Lazy Jack. The trouble was, I just didn't like working.

Jill said to me, 'There's not been a giant round here for years. You've got to do something instead of just sitting around all day.'

'Like what?' I asked.

'I've heard they're looking for fishermen down at the harbour. The fishing trade is booming. Why don't you go and try to get a job on one of the boats?'

'Oh, but I don't like fish,' I moaned. 'They're all wriggly and slimy, and they haven't got any eyelids – they look at you all the time. Blurgh! No, I don't like fish.'

'Go and be a fisherman. I'm sick of you moping around all day. It'll be an adventure!' Jill shouted.

I went down the mountain and trudged down the road towards the harbour. Once there, I soon got a job on board a boat and was out to sea that same day. But to be honest, I was a useless fisherman. I had thrown my rod into the water as soon as I had caught a fish as I didn't like the way it looked at me.

Then the captain of the boat gave me a net to see if I'd get on any better with that. In no time at all I had caught a huge ball of mackerel. I hauled the net onto the deck of the boat and opened it up. The mackerel danced and flitted around the deck and there in middle of these jumping fish was a fine salmon. This fish didn't move, it lay perfectly still and seemed to be looking up at me.

'I can't kill this animal. It's beautiful!' I thought.

I then picked up the salmon, made sure no one was looking, leant over the side of the boat and let the fish go. It disappeared into the water, but not before it made a 'plop' sound.

'Are you throwing away my haul?' bellowed the captain. 'That's it. I've had enough, Jack! You're sacked.'

Once back at the harbour, I trudged slowly along the road home. As soon as I got through the door, Jill looked at me and said, 'What happened?'

'I'm not good at fishing. I'm only good at giant killing,' I sighed.

'But we've run out of money,' Jill explained to me. 'We've lived on this mountain for years and we've run out of everything. Here, take my ring. Head down to the market and sell it.'

'I can't sell your ring!' I exclaimed. 'It belonged to your father.'

'You must sell the ring or we'll starve,' Jill said sadly.

I took the ring and trudged once more down the mountain. As I walked, I wondered what we might do next. Maybe I would meet a giant who I could kill. Maybe I'd be rewarded and we would be rich once more. I was lost in thought when I bumped into a tall man.

'Oh, I'm terribly sorry. I didn't see you,' I apologised.

'That's quite all right, Jack,' the man smiled.

This tall man was dressed in a fine black suit. He was wearing a top hat, carried a cane and had a dark goatee beard.

'How do you know my name?' I asked.

The man flashed a dazzling smile and his green eyes burnt a brighter green. He spoke in smooth and silky tones.

'I know a lot about you. I know you are having money trouble. Perhaps I can be of assistance. Perhaps you would like to loan my cow?'

The man clicked his fingers and there standing in the middle of the road was a fine Jersey cow with bulging udders that needed milking right away.

'Wow!' blurted Jack. 'I'd love to loan your cow. That's a healthy-looking animal, that. Jill would be delighted if I came home a dairy farmer. But what do you want from me?'

'Oh, nothing much,' smiled the man. 'You can loan my cow for, let's say, one year. At the end of the year, I'll come back and ask you three questions. If you get the questions right, you can keep the cow. If you get the questions wrong, *then I'll take your soul*!'

'That's sounds like an excellent idea,' I laughed. 'You've got a deal.'

I shook hands with the man and took the cow by her collar up the mountain.

'Blimey, Jack!' said Jill. 'You've done well there. That cow for my ring?'

'Even better!' I laughed. 'Here's your ring back. I met a man who has loaned us this cow for a year. At the end of the year, he'll ask me three questions. If I get them right, we keep the cow! Good, eh?'

'What if you get them wrong?' asked Jill suspiciously.

'Then he takes my soul.'

'*What*? I don't mean to be rude, Jack, but you're an idiot. That man was the devil. There's no way you'll get three questions right. You've sold your soul – for a cow!'

'Then I shall go to the library!' I said suddenly. 'I shall read books and make myself clever.'

I went off to the library every day. I read book after book after book. It was the hardest I had ever worked in my life.

Meanwhile, Jill milked the cow every day and turned their house into a café. There she sold milk, butter, cheese, yoghurt. And she even invented something called the milkshake. People loved the milkshake and came from miles around to taste it.

But, once the year was over, I came home from the library and said, 'Well, Jill, time is up. Today is the day the devil comes to ask his three questions.'

'Oh, Jack!' she sobbed. 'I can't watch.'

I stood behind the counter of the café. I looked around and saw that it was practically deserted. There was just one stranger sitting in a corner. He had a hood pulled over his head and had only a glass of water in front of him. Suddenly, the devil appeared with a flash in front of me.

'Hello, Jack!' smiled the devil. 'Are you ready for your three questions?'

'Yes,' I answered. 'Yes, I am ready.'

The stranger in the corner of the café leapt to his feet and bellowed, '*That* was your first question!'

'What?' spluttered the devil. 'What's going on here, Jack?'

'I don't know what's going on, I swear!' I answered.

'*That* is your second question!' boomed the stranger.

'Who is that man, Jack?' demanded the devil.

'I don't know, I've never seen him before!' I answered.

'And *that* is your third question!' roared the stranger. 'You've had your three questions and you've had your three answers, now be gone with you, devil!'

The devil's face flashed a scarlet colour, his eyes glowed emerald green, he stamped his foot on the ground and disappeared into a puff of dark grey smoke.

I turned to the stranger and asked, 'Who are you?'

The stranger lowered his hood as he moved towards me. His skin had a silvery sheen to it, his eyes were perfectly round and he had no eyelids. On his neck were three lines on one side and three lines on the other.

'I am the King of the Fishes,' the stranger said. 'One year ago you saved my life. Now I have returned to save yours – use it wisely, Jack.'

With that, the stranger turned and walked out of the café. I ran to tell Jill all that had happened. We had the cow and we would be happy.

But the devil has a habit of holding grudges and I would soon meet him again.

About this story

In the Bible, the devil tried to tempt Jesus by asking three questions. This story is likely to be based on that. Three is a number frequently used in myths, legends, folk and fairy tales. As well as having three characters, such as three pigs or three billy goats, three events might happen such as eating porridge, sitting in chairs and sleeping in beds. This pattern of using three things is known as a triadic structure.

Teaching idea: Triadic structure

The devil asked three questions and Jack gave three correct answers. But these questions were really rhetorical and didn't need Jack to answer them.

1. 'Are you ready for your three questions?'

2. 'What's going on here?'

3. 'Who is that man?'

Characters like the Mad Hatter in *Alice in Wonderland* ask nonsensical questions such as, 'Why is a raven like a writing desk?'

Alice replies, 'What's the answer?'

The Mad Hatter says, 'I haven't the slightest idea.'

The question was silly and rhetorical as there was no answer to give. Ask the children a series of questions such as:

- Do fish get thirsty?

- Why do your feet smell and why does your nose run?

- What colour is Friday?

- If you paint a window black, is it still a window?

- Is lined paper heavier than plain paper?

- Can a dog really be your friend?

- Can you cry underwater?

- If a bookshop has no books, is it still a bookshop?

- What colour is a glass of seawater?

- If a clock stops, is it still a clock?

These questions are interpretative and can be a good source of classroom discussion. They are based upon Ian Gilbert's book, *The Little Book of Thunks: 260 questions to make your brain go ouch!*. The questions encourage you to look at everyday things in new and challenging ways. There are no right or wrong answers; they are only your own and other people's opinions.

After discussing the questions and any possible answers in partners, small groups and as a class, ask the children to come up with their own questions. You could give them prompts such as:

- Can a tiger ever . . . ?

- Would a baby . . . ?

- Which came first . . . ?

- Can you use an egg to . . . ?

- Do shadows . . . ?

- Is the dark side of the moon . . . ?

- Would you rather . . . ?

- If a tree . . . ?

- Is it ever right to . . . ?

- Is it always wrong to . . . ?

These questions could be shared and discussed, too. The children could then select their favourite three questions, either the ones they have created themselves or ones they have enjoyed discussing. The questions could then be used in a narrative trickster story in the same style as the one above. A devil or demon character could ask the main character the questions and the children have to work out creative ways of answering. For example:

The demon asked, 'Would a baby ever win an arm-wrestling competition?'

'Yes,' I replied. 'There is no time limit set, so the baby can grow up to become strong.'

The demon then asked, 'If a tree is chopped down, is it still just wood?'

'No,' I replied. 'It can be a pencil, a chair, a box, a book or anything we can imagine it to be.'

The demon finally asked, 'Is it ever right to steal?'

'Yes,' I replied. 'If it means saving a life such as feeding the starving.'

This style of writing means that the children have to justify their own opinions and begin to express themselves in their writing using their own written voice, so becoming confident, independent writers. But they need opportunities to express these opinions orally before moving on to the writing stage.

16 Abhartach the vampire (Irish)

In Derry there is a place near to Slaghtaverty called 'Giant's Cave', which is an ironic name, as the creature that haunted the land was an undead dwarf. Some call the place 'Abhartach's Sepulchre' as it is the grave of the vampiric creature from this story. His name Abhartach comes from the word 'abhac' which means 'dwarf'. The name of the chieftain who battles the dwarf is Cathán. This name comes from the word 'cath' which means 'battle'. Evil creatures that were undead were known as 'neamhmairbh', meaning 'undead'. These creatures were all said to have 'bad blood', which is what made them return from the dead. If you translate the phrase 'bad blood' into Irish, it is 'droch fhola', pronounced 'drocula', which sounds a lot like 'Dracula'. It is believed that Bram Stoker took inspiration from the legend of Abhartach for his novel Dracula *after studying in Ireland.*

Abhartach the vampire

Long ago, near Derry, there was a town named Slaghtaverty which had a hillfort nearby that none of the townsfolk went near. It was a place abandoned by humans, but a pack of wolves had moved in. They howled ferociously every full moon, which sent shivers down anyone's spine who heard the bloodcurdling call.

The hillfort had once belonged to an evil warlord named Abhartach. He had been a dwarf and the son of a poet but, unlike his father who was gentle and kind, Abhartach was a cruel and vicious man. He had tortured and killed dozens of people until at last he was defeated in battle.

However, even after his death people had seen a dwarf-like creature lurking in the shadows beneath the fort. This creature could turn himself into any animal and could even turn invisible, too. He would leap upon unsuspecting travellers and drink their blood, but no bodies were ever found as the creature would drag the lifeless victims back to the hillfort and feed the corpses to the wolves. People believed that the creature was Abhartach returned from the dead.

Eventually, the people of Slaghtaverty called upon their chieftain Cathán to do something about Abhartach. Cathán was strong, brave and a great warrior. He thought that a blood-sucking dwarf would be no match for him! But Cathán was also clever. He had heard of Abhartach's magical abilities, so Cathán decided not to race into battle with a sorcerer but rather to go and watch the hillfort to study Abhartach's nightly movements.

One full moon, as the wolves howled and the wind gusted, Cathán remained hidden among some trees. His narrow eyes watched the hillfort carefully. There was a patch of freshly dug soil below the fort. It was rectangular and about the size of a small coffin. The mud was mounded up and glowed darkly. As the wolves went off to hunt for prey, the soil began to move. It rumbled as though there was an earthquake, then a hand emerged from the soft soil. It clawed at the night sky. Cathán knew this was the undead dwarf. He sprinted towards the hand before the rest of the body could emerge. He unsheathed his sword and plunged it down into the ground. There was a choked cry from beneath the earth and blood spewed up like a fountain.

Cathán pulled free his sword. There was another muffled scream, then Abhartach reached up another hand. He suddenly sat up from the grave, sending soil flying in all directions. His face was twisted into a contorted mask of fury. Cathán lunged his sword into the dwarf's chest and the screaming howl stopped. Abhartach slumped backwards and was dead once more.

Cathán pulled up the body from the soil. He couldn't bear to look at the dwarf's face. It was the most grotesque thing he had ever seen in his life. So Cathán pulled the cloak that Abhartach was wearing over his face then heaved up the body. Cathán rested the corpse on his shoulder and carried it off to be buried far from the town under heavy rocks. The chieftain was built like a mountain and he effortlessly carried boulder after boulder, then heaped them on top of the twice-dead Abhartach.

Cathán went home exhausted and went to sleep for what remained of the night, feeling satisfied that he had rid the townsfolk of the terrible undead monster. But the following night two people went missing. Then three people disappeared the night after that. The townsfolk banged at Cathán's door, crying in terror.

The huge chieftain set off with his sword to where he had buried Abhartach and there, beyond the boulders piled high, was a mountain. Cathán waited until nightfall, then watched and waited again. Sure enough, through a small gap in the mountainside Abhartach emerged. He was small, stooped and cloaked in black. The hood was down and the face was even more terrifying than Cathán remembered. The undead dwarf set off towards the town.

Cathán was a huge man, but he could move stealthily. He stalked behind Abhartach and silently drew his sword. Cathán crept ever closer, then, when he was close enough to strike, the chieftain brought down his sword and Abhartach slumped to the floor dead again.

Cathán carried the body to the cave and threw it inside. Then he carried boulders again, but sealed the body inside this time. There would be no escape from that! But Cathán had forgotten about Abhartach's shape-shifting powers. The undead creature had returned the next night, transformed into a spider and scuttled free from the rocky tomb. Then he feasted on a whole herd of cows, their lifeless bodies left strewn around a field.

The furious farmers banged at Cathán's door. The chieftain knew that he needed help, so he went to find the druid of the woods.

The druid lived in a cabin in a clearing deep inside a woodland area. Cathán knocked at the door and it opened to reveal a tall, slender man with an impossibly long white beard.

'You're here about Abhartach,' the druid announced.

'I am and I bring you this.'

The chieftain offered the druid a bag of silver.

'I can help you, but in return I do not seek silver. You will be in debt to me. You will owe me a favour. Agreed?'

The chieftain nodded quickly.

'You are trying to kill that which is already dead. It is now *neamhmairbh*, the walking dead. Your iron sword is no good against those who do not live. Instead, make a sword from the wood of a yew tree. Drive it through the monster's heart and bury him upside down so that he faces hell instead of heaven, then fill the grave with clay and rocks. Finally, place a ring of thorns around the grave and only that will stop the undead creature.'

Cathán nodded and thanked the druid. Then the chieftain cut down a yew tree on his way from the woods. He also gathered the thorns from a hawthorn bush. When he got home, he carved and whittled for the rest of the day until he had made a sword from yew.

That night, Cathán returned to the rocky mountain and waited. Abhartach was a black snake that slithered from the cave and then turned into the hunched, hooded figure. Cathán was horrified by the grotesque face again, but dared not turn away.

The chieftain followed the dwarf over the rocks. Cathán was a silent predator stalking his prey. When he was upon the undead creature, he cried out a might battle roar. Abhartach spun around and Cathán stabbed him with his yew sword. The wood pierced the dwarf's heart. He screamed and slumped to the floor dead again. But would this be the last time?

Cathán covered the hideous face, then picked up the body. He carried it back to the hillfort. Using his iron sword, he dug away the soft soil from where Abhartach had emerged that first night, then he put the body inside, making sure it was facing downwards. The chieftain filled the grave with soft clay soil and large rocks that were dotted around the place. Once the body was completely buried, Cathán pulled a leather sack from his belt that held the thorns. He made a large circle around the grave with the thorns and then stepped back.

He had done all that the druid had said, but would it be enough to stop the undead from rising? The nights that followed seemed to show that it would. There were no travellers drained of blood and no cattle with their throats cut left in the fields. Even the wolves that lived in the hillfort left to find a new home. Cathán had defeated the undead and the land was safe. But the druid would soon call upon Cathán to fight more *neamhmairbh*. But that is a story for another time.

Teaching idea: Describing a character

Abhartach's face is described in the story as grotesque, terrifying and hideous, but other than these three adjectives, there is very little description. Ask the children to imagine a face that is 'grotesque, terrifying and hideous', then tell each other what this face would look like. They should consider the hair, forehead, eyes, nose, mouth, chin, ears, skin and neck. You could then write some descriptive phrases on the board to inspire further descriptions such as:

- disfigured and warped

- demonic expression

- hollow, empty, gaping sockets

- twisted lips

- haunted eyes

- hairy and warty

- pig-like snout

- wide, bulbous nose

- ravaged by time

- deathly ink-black

- deep folds

- knotted, lice-ridden hair

- sharp teeth like knives

- blood-splattered

- toothless hag

- pointed ears

- deeply creased

- gnarled and twisted

- patches of hair

- sinisterly staring

Abhartach is later described as 'small, stooped and cloaked in black' and was 'hunched and hooded'. Ask the children to describe what Abhartach's body might have looked like.

Ask them to consider the shoulders, torso, arms, legs, fingers, toes, knees, elbows, clothes, shoes and posture. Ask them to also discuss how he might move. They could act this out before the discussion, too. You could write further descriptive phrases to help such as:

- tattered cloak

- shrouded in a cavernous hood

- enveloped his body

- flapped in the cold night

- veiny and mottled

- humped and stooped

- jagged fingernails

- ancient and evil

- crept silently

- stalked stealthily

- rough and scratchy

- juddering steps

- wiry body hairs sprouting all over

- warty and calloused

- bloated, bulging belly

- weather worn

- decomposing flesh

- hideous stench

- monstrous and sinister

- sharpened like daggers

Once the children have described how they imagined Abhartach's appearance, they could then draw sketches of the vampiric dwarf and label them with the descriptive phrases that you gave them, ones of their own or a mixture of the two.

Then ask the children to write descriptions by turning these phrases into full sentences. You could model the first few sentences to give them something to start with. For example:

Abhartach wore a **demonic expression** with **haunted eyes**. He had a **wide, bulbous nose** below **deathly ink black** eyes. This **ancient and evil** vampire walked in **juddering steps** on toenails **sharpened like daggers**.

By highlighting the descriptive phrases used, you are showing children how they can be inserted in sentences. They could then use the same structure with their own descriptive phrases.

The children could then design and describe their own *neamhmairbh* characters such as zombies, werewolves, demons, witches, etc.

17 Tammy and the trows (Scottish)

The Shetland Islands are the northernmost part of the United Kingdom. The islands are located 106 miles north of Scotland and 143 miles west of Norway. Stories from Shetland feature major influences from Norse mythology, including giant sea monsters and trows. In this tale, there is a family of trows that live inside a hill. Trows are similar to trolls, which have featured in popular franchises such as in Frozen and The Lord of the Rings, but their origin comes from Nordic oral storytelling. In Viking tales of trolls, the creatures always came from wild landscapes such as forests, caves or mountains. The landscape of Shetland is a perfect place for these troll-like creatures. Trows are nocturnal and have a taste for human flesh, as we shall see in the tale below.

Tammy and the trows

Tammy lived in a village at the bottom of a large hill. The hill was named Trow Hill, so-called because a family of trows lived deep inside. Nobody from the village went out of their houses at night for fear that the trows would get them. Trows would eat people, especially children. They loved cooked children!

But Tammy would never listen to anyone. His father had told him never to walk on the slippery stones down by the river. His mother told him that if he did, then he would fall in. But Tammy played down by the river anyway. He skipped over the stones to cross to the other side, but fell into the freezing and deep water. He had a cold for a week after that.

One day, Tammy collected his ball and was bouncing it around the house. He knocked over a lamp, smashed a mug and toppled a chair.

'Enough!' his dad shouted.

'Go play with your friends!' his mother bellowed.

Tammy smiled and nodded.

'Make sure you're back by dark,' his parents had said together. 'Watch out for the trows!'

'Trows!' laughed Tammy as he sped out of the house and into the village. 'There's no such thing as trows.'

Tammy walked up and down the streets, looking for his friends to play with. He thought about going to their houses, but then he looked up at the hill. There was an old abandoned house way up there. He'd been meaning to check it out several times. Maybe today should be the day?

He chuckled. He'd bring back a souvenir to show his friends. So, bouncing his ball and wearing a smile as wide as a river, he was off. He bounded up the hill. It was bigger than he thought, though. He threw and kicked his ball against large rocks until, at last, he came to the rickety old house. It was almost dark by the time he had reached it. He thought about going back home, but he had come all this way. He looked at the house. It had was a ramshackle place held up by luck and wishes. The walls were crumbling, the windows were cracked and the door hung on its hinges, but there was smoke coming from the chimney.

Tammy got closer and peered through the dirt-smeared window. There were voices coming from inside.

Roasted girls and toasted boys,

Boil them in oil to stop their noise.

The song was being chanted by rasping, hoarse voices. Tammy could make out three hunched figures around a table. There was a roaring fire and several candles dotted around the room, but the window was so grimy that he couldn't quite make out who the figures were. Was it Old Jimmy the butcher and his mates?

Tammy went to the swinging front door and peered inside. Just then one of the figures saw him. Tammy gasped. A huge warty and hairy creature burst through the doorframe. It could barely fit as it was as wide as it was tall.

'What have we here?' croaked the figure.

Tammy was lifted up and the creature narrowed its yellow eyes into slits.

'A boy!'

The breath of the creature was hot enough to melt rocks. There was a metallic tang to it, too, like blood. The skin was green and rough.

'Hello!' Tammy said and tried his charming smile.

'Look what was outside our door!'

The other two figures turned to see and Tammy gasped again. Trows were real, after all. The three trows grinned at him, revealing long, sharp teeth and snake-like black tongues.

'Breakfast!' barked one trow.

'But it's bedtime. You won't sleep a wink with me in your belly!' Tammy said quickly.

'We're just up,' the trow replied. 'You'll be tasty fried in butter!'

Tammy noticed a massive dog with flaming red eyes sitting by the fire. The trow dog began to growl at the boy.

'Shut up!' snapped the trow and kicked the dog.

'Let's just boil him!' another trow suggested.

The third trow prodded Tammy.

'He's nice and plump. He might be better chopped up in our porridge.'

'You don't want to eat me!' Tammy butted in. 'I'm all gristle and bone. I'll give you stomach-ache.'

The three trows laughed and the trow dog howled.

'They all say that,' one trow said with a grin.

'Until they start screaming,' added another.

'Then they go quiet,' the third smiled.

'You're right,' smiled Tammy. 'I'll be very tasty indeed.'

The trows seemed happy with this and pushed Tammy into a chair. They each grabbed a knife and began sharpening the blades.

'But can I suggest you put me in a pie?'

The trows stopped and looked at Tammy.

'If you have an onion and add a bit of sage, then I'd be lovely in a pie. Imagine that. A golden, crumbly crust and succulent boy underneath. What do you think?'

Drool began to run from the corners of the trows' mouths.

'That does sound nice,' one said.

'We haven't had pie in ages,' added another.

'Yeah, all right, then,' the third agreed.

'I'll make the pastry,' the first trow said. 'You go get the onion and you go get the sage.'

The two trows agreed and shuffled out of the cottage and down the hill towards the village. After they'd been gone a few minutes and the remaining trow was busy mixing flour and butter, Tammy coughed.

'Sorry to bother you,' he said. 'But have you any bay leaves?'

'No, why?' snapped the trow.

'My grandmother reckons that a pie just doesn't taste the same without a bay leaf. Parsley, too. It just gives the meat that tasty, juicy quality. It melts in your mouth with the gravy.'

The trow began to drool again.

'You're right,' the trow said. 'I'm off to go and get some. But don't you think about leaving while I'm gone. My dog here will tear you to pieces if you do!'

The dog began to growl in agreement.

'I'm not going anywhere. I'm tired.' Tammy yawned and stretched back into the chair.

The trow seemed satisfied and set off. After a few minutes, Tammy jumped up from the chair. The dog growled again. He took a few steps towards the door, but the dog leapt up and blocked his way. Its eyes burned red and its teeth were bared.

Tammy got out the ball he had been playing with and began to bounce it up and down, over and over again. The dog's red eyes followed it, then its tongue lolled to one side. Tammy passed the ball from one hand to the other. The dog barked with excitement. Tammy then opened the door and threw the ball as hard as he could away from the house.

Tammy then raced in the opposite direction down the hill as fast as his legs would carry him. He raced like a mountain goat leaping over rocks and bounding over boulders. At last, he reached the bottom. Breathless and panting, he walked into the village and gave a long, deep outward breath.

'That was close!' he sighed, then smiled. 'Too close!'

'Oi!' came a thunderous cry. 'What are you doing down here?'

Tammy turned to see the three trows running towards him. They were huge and lumbering, yet they moved very quickly. Tammy turned and ran straight towards the river. He sprinted to the riverbank and leapt onto the stones. He skipped from one stone to the next and soon had crossed to the other side. The trows followed, but as they approached the middle, the first trow slipped and flailed its arms in the air. It fell backwards into the other two trows and they all fell down into the water. Their arms churned in the deep water and then they sank below the dark depths.

Tammy ran home and told his parents everything that had happened. They hugged him close and put him to bed with a steaming mug of cocoa.

About this story

The trows in the story lived in a house, on a hill, on an island. Ask the children to design their own islands. They could add their own features such as hills, rivers, volcanoes, swamps, forests, caves, beaches, waterfalls, etc. The children could then choose one location where a family of trows or trolls might live. The children could design and describe these characters, too.

Tammy escapes from the trolls by using his quick wits and knowledge of the island where he lives. The children could plan an action scene of how they could escape from the trolls on their island. They could use a storyboard to do this, so that the action is planned pictorially but then written up using the storyboard as a guide.

Teaching idea: Storyboards

Storyboard created by Isla McAllister

The sample storyboard here shows Tammy's escape in six boxes.

1. Tammy runs from the trows through a forest.

2. He arrives in town and thinks he has escaped them.

3. The trows arrive in town.

4. Tammy runs to the river and the trows are in pursuit.

5. The trows slip on the stones and fall into the river.

6. Tammy has escaped.

This sample storyboard retells the events in the story. However, the children could use the same structure to plan a new action scene. Instead of escaping the trows, the children could trap them. By physically making the traps, the children should be able to retell what they did, thus making the descriptions more vivid.

Perhaps the children could also use natural materials from their island to trap the trows. Gather some sticks from a woodland area to be taken into school. Make sure you have some Y-shaped sticks as these can form the base for the trap. You might also collect fern leaves, too, to make the traps camouflage.

Show the children your collected sticks and ferns, and explain that the children are going to work outdoors to build their own trow traps. The children could then work in teams to collect more natural materials from the school grounds. This activity is best done in autumn when a range of leaves can be used. The children could also collect moss, dried grass, stones, feathers, bark, etc. It is worthwhile telling the children not to pick anything that is still growing and also not to pick mushrooms or berries.

The children could begin their traps by pushing a Y-shaped stick into the ground diagonally. Other sticks could then rest on this Y-shaped stick to form a frame like a tepee. The other natural materials could then go around the trap to camouflage it.

There might be features such as when you pull a certain stick, the whole structure collapses on the trow, trapping it inside. There might be a lure or bait to entice the trow inside, or perhaps there is a pit dug inside the trap itself. Let the children come up with their own ideas working collaboratively in teams.

Once the traps have been assembled, the children could use a storyboard to show how the trows have been trapped. These could be turned into descriptions later.

18 The king's secret (Welsh)

This story is about a king named March ap Meirchion. In English, this name means 'Stallion son of stallions' which is a fitting name, for the king had a secret that directly relates to his name. The king was ashamed of his secret and kept it hidden for as long as he could. The story is almost identical to an Ancient Greek myth in which King Midas (famous for his 'golden touch') declared that the god Pan could play better music than the god Apollo. Enraged by this, Apollo cursed Midas and gave him donkey's ears. The king hid his ears beneath a turban like King March hid his underneath a crown. The narrative then follows much the same as this story from Wales.

The king's secret

In the Welsh valleys there was a travelling barber. He went from place to place seeing the sights and meeting people. One day, he arrived at a town he had never visited before. He spent the day walking the streets until he arrived at the market place. There, he saw the king of that town, King March ap Meirchion, riding past on a magnificent stallion. The king was dressed in luxurious robes and on top of his head he wore a gigantic crown that covered the side and the top of his head.

The barber became curious about the oversized crown. He went to a tavern, ordered a drink and said to the barman, 'Excuse me, but why does your king wear such a large crown?'

'*Ssshhh*!' screeched the barman. 'Don't mention the crown! King March is very sensitive about it. He never takes it off and if anyone questions him about it, they are immediately thrown into the dungeon to rot. Don't mention the turban – *ever*!'

This made the barber even more curious and eventually he worked in King March's palace cutting the servants' hair. The barber was most excellent at his job and the king soon noticed the fancy new haircuts his servants had. So the king ordered the barber to cut his majesty's hair the next day.

The barber knocked and waited at the door of the king's bedroom.

'Enter.'

He opened the door and bowed low.

'You may approach.'

The barber walked slowly forward. His leather apron had his scissors, razor blade, brushes, combs, oils and creams. The king was seated in front of a mirror at a dressing table. He slowly took off the crown.

'What you see next, you must never tell anyone about.'

The barber nodded, curious as to what would happen next. The king continued to lift the crown and revealed a thick head of dark hair. All seemed ordinary enough until he saw the king's ears flopping out from behind the hair. The barber let out a little gasp. The king had the ears of a horse.

'Understood?' asked King March.

The barber nodded quickly with wide eyes. He then began to comb the king's hair with care. The scissors snipped and the razor blade shaved. Soon the hair cut was complete and the barber left the palace. He raced straight to the tavern he had been to previously.

'Barman,' said the barber. 'Give me a drink quickly. I've had quite a shock! I know why your king wears that large crown. You see King March – '

'*Ssshhh*!' screeched the barman. 'Don't mention the crown! I've told you before. I don't want to know why he wears it. I want to stay out of the dungeon.'

The barber bit his lip. He felt that this secret would burst out of him if he didn't tell even just one person.

'B– but I've got to tell someone,' moaned the barber.

'Well,' said the barman. 'Why don't you go down to the riverbank, dig a hole and shout the secret into the hole. It'll make you feel better.'

The barber rushed to the riverbank and arrived at a swampy bog. Here the reeds grew tall and strong. The ground was soft and the barber dug a hole with his hands like a dog. When it was about the size of a bucket, the barber put his head inside the hole and shouted:

'King March has got horse's ears!'

The barber smiled and sighed. It was such a relief to shout out the secret that he did it again:

'King March has got horse's ears!'

He shouted it again and again and again:

'King March has got horse's ears!'

'King March has got horse's ears!'

'King March has got horse's ears!'

After the barber had shouted out the secret many times, he went back to the palace to finish cutting the servant's hair. Eventually, the barber decided to move on to another valley to carry on exploring.

Many years passed. King March's birthday was coming up and he wanted to throw a party in his palace. Everyone in the town was to be invited. So the king sent for his musicians and said, 'Musicians, I want you to compose a piece of music about how wonderful I am. I want you to perform this at my birthday party to everyone.'

'Of course, your majesty,' said the musicians, bowing low.

But as soon as the king had left them on their own, they looked at each other and said, 'How are we going to do that? The king is mean and nasty all the time. He's always throwing people into the dungeon and leaving them to rot. How can we fill a whole song about how wonderful he is?'

'I know!' said the piper. 'I'll perform a long bagpipe solo in the middle of the song. That will take up some time.'

The musicians all agreed and began to compose the song immediately.

A few days passed and the day of the party had finally arrived. Everyone was gathered at the palace. The musicians began to get very nervous. No one was more nervous than the piper. He paced around the room and eventually put his pipes down onto a stool to get a drink from the buffet table. A few people brushed passed the stool and knocked the pipes to the floor. The bag sat deflated with the chanter and reed sticking out.

When the piper walked back to the rest of the musicians, he stepped onto his pipes and with a *crack* the reed snapped in two.

'Oh no!' exclaimed the piper. 'The reed! I can't play the pipes without the reed!'

'What does it do?' asked one of the musicians.

'It's the bit you blow into,' the piper answered. 'But, hang on, I might just have time to make a new one!'

So the piper ran down to the riverbank, took out his penknife, cut a tall reed that was growing there and carved it into a mouthpiece for his pipes. He then rushed back to the party, but he had no time to test his pipes as the musicians were about to perform their song. He pushed the new reed into the chanter just as King March sat on his throne and nodded to the musicians to begin.

'King March is a marvellous! King March is epic! King March is brave!'

'King March is wonderful! King March is awesome! King March is strong!'

This went on for a bit and then it was almost time for the piper to play his solo. He blew into the reed to inflate the bag and started to move his fingers up and down the chanter. There was a dull droning sound, followed by the high-pitched squeak of the pipes that screeched:

> *'King March has got horse's ears!'*

The piper stopped. The musicians gasped. The crowd stared. King March glared and said:

'What did you just say? Play it again!'

'King March is marvellous! King March is epic! King March is brave!'

'King March is wonderful! King March is awesome! King March is strong!'

The piper then brought the reed to his lips, blew into it and out came:

> *'King March has got horse's ears!'*

'Take that man away and throw him into the dungeon to rot!' barked the king.

'W— w— what?' stammered the piper. 'B— b— but it wasn't me. It was the pipes!'

'Ha! The pipes?' scoffed King March. 'Bring them to me!'

The piper handed the pipes to the king. He brought the reed to his lips, blew into it and the sound came out:

'*King March has got horse's ears*!'

The king leapt to his feet and shouted:

'How is this possible? I want everyone here questioned until I get the answer!'

The king's guards questioned everyone at the party and eventually the barman was brought forward to King March.

The barman said: 'Y— your majesty. I once met a travelling barber who said that he knew why you wore your large crown. I told him not to tell anyone but rather he should dig a hole in the riverbank and shout the secret into it. That reed from the pipes must have grown at the riverbank and held the secret inside it – until someone blew into it and realised the secret for all to hear.'

King March thought about this for moment or two.

Then the barman said, 'We all know your secret now, your majesty. Can we look at your horse's ears?'

King March nodded, then slowly began to take off his oversized crown. The horse's ears flopped out for all to see.

'I like them,' said the barman. 'I don't like my ears, though. They're like saucers on my head. They're too big.'

Suddenly someone at the back of the room shouted, 'And I don't like my fingers. They look like spoons!'

Then some else called out, 'I don't like my nose – it's like a bird's beak!'

'And I've got a birthmark on my bum!'

King March soon realised that we all have things about ourselves that we don't like. He stopped wearing the oversized crown and let his horse's ears flop out for all to see. He became a much nicer person and stopped throwing people into the dungeon to rot.

In fact, horse's ears became so fashionable in that town that they used to sell them on the market place for people to wear on their heads. From that day on, everyone in town lived happily ever after.

About this story

This story contains a lot of dialogue at the end when the secret is revealed and the king takes off his crown. King March does not expect the reaction of the crowd, especially when they reveal what they don't like about themselves. We can use this part of the story as a model to write some dialogue in the classroom.

Teaching idea: Writing dialogue

Ask the children to choose an animal's facial feature to replace one of their own facial features. It could be elephant's ears, spider's eyes, shark's mouth, pig's nose, snake's tongue, sheep's hair or giraffe's neck. The children could then write an exclamation such as:

'I've got chameleon's eyes!'

The children could then choose a verb instead of 'said'. As this is an exclamation, it could be 'exclaimed'. It could also be shouted, screamed, shrieked, bellowed, announced, boasted, yelled, etc. Ask the children to then add an adverb to the verb, such as loudly, suddenly, noisily, confidently, deafeningly, boldly, thunderously, etc.

The children could then go on to describe their unique facial features with adjectives. The reason we have chosen facial features is that it follows the model in the text, but also avoids body parts such as bums.

With their verbs, adverbs and adjectives, the children could then write more descriptive dialogue, such as:

'I've got chameleon's eyes!' I announced confidently. 'They're huge, round and weird.'

Prepositions could also be added, using phrases that begin with beneath, beside, next to, near, above, underneath, on top of, etc. For example:

'I've got chameleon's eyes!' I announced confidently. 'They're huge, round and weird. They're above my nose and between my ears on my face.'

More adjectives could then be added to describe the children's faces. They could use adjectives like smooth, long, shiny, handsome, beautiful, cute, pretty, etc. They might write something like:

'I've got massive chameleon's eyes!' I announced confidently. 'They're huge, round and weird. They are above my cute nose and between my long ears on my handsome face.'

This same model could then be used for other characters, such as family members, friends and teachers, or characters from books, film, TV or video games. For example:

'Well, that's nothing!' Mr Bushnell declared quickly. 'I've got an eagle's beak for a nose! It's long, sharp and deadly. It's in the centre of my round face, below my shining eyes and above my smiling mouth.'

'You think that's weird?' boomed Snow White. 'I've got bird's wings for ears! They're fluffy, soft and blue. They are at the side of straight hair, beside my twinkling eyes and above my rounded chin.'

'Oh, yeah?' laughed Sonic the Hedgehog. 'Well, I've got snail's eyes! They're gigantic, slimy and yellow. They loom above my spiky hair, towering over my tiny nose and way above my fast feet.'

The children could use hyperbole to describe their own and other pupils' facial features. A range of punctuation could also be explored, as modelled in the sentences above.

19 Jack-o'-lantern (Irish)

This final Jack story comes from Ireland. We still see the familiar character traits that the English Jack employs throughout his exploits such as laziness combined with wit and luck, but there is also something tragic about this tale. This is the end of Jack's days and tells the origin of pumpkin carving. In Ireland and then in Scotland and beyond, people carved their own versions of Jack lanterns. However, it was turnips and potatoes that were carved. In England, people carved beetroots. It was only when people from the UK travelled to America and took the tradition with them, that pumpkins, which are native to America, were then used. Pumpkins are much easier to carve, so the tradition evolved into what we know today.

Jack-o'-lantern

Jack was on his way home from the pub when he passed the local graveyard. Just then, a swirling white mist rose up from one of the graves and began to take shape in the air. The mist became a white ghostly figure who whispered, 'Woo . . . Wooooo . . . Wooooooooo!'

The ghost opened its mouth impossibly wide. It got closer and closer to Jack, all the while whispering. But the whispering turned into a howling and it hovered right above Jack's head.

'Woo . . . Wooooo . . . Wooooooooo!'

The mouth opened wider still and the ghost hovered and glared down at Jack.

'All right there, mate!' said Jack. 'How are you tonight, then?'

He smiled and waved at the ghost. The ghost stared back at him. It closed its mouth and floated to the floor. The expression changed from an angry one to something soft and calm. It eventually rasped, '*You are the first person to speak to me in over a hundred years. For that reason, I will grant you three wishes.*'

'Three wishes!' exclaimed Jack. 'What will I wish for? Erm, I know! My wife, Jill, is always sending me off for firewood and every time I fill up my sack, I always trip over and drop the wood all over the floor. So, I wish that whatever I put in my sack has to stay in there until I give it permission to get out.'

'That's a strange wish,' mused the ghost. 'What else do you wish for?'

'Erm, what next? Oh, I know! I have a lovely apple tree in my garden, but every time the fruit is ripe and I go to pick an apple, they're gone! The children in my village are always stealing them. Scrumping my apples, that's what they do. I wish that whoever grabs on to one of my apples won't be able to let go unless I give permission.'

'Hmmm, strange indeed,' said the ghost. 'But have it your way. What's your final wish?'

'Erm, all right, then. What else bothers me now? Ah! Jill is always inviting people into our house. Every time I get in from the pub or from gathering wood, there's always someone sitting in my armchair. I wish that whoever sits in my armchair won't be able to get up unless I give them permission.'

'You're a very strange man, Jack,' said the ghost and then disappeared into a white mist once more.

Jack shrugged his shoulders and made his way home. In the morning Jill sent him out for firewood. While collecting the wood he suddenly screamed, '*Owwww*! I've got a splinter in my finger! *Owwww*!'

Jack ran home and showed Jill the splinter. He writhed on the floor in pain. Jill got a needle and tried to get the splinter out, but '*Ooooooowwwwwww*!' Jack screeched. 'You've made it even worse now! You pushed it right under the nail. Oh, I'd give anything to take away the pain!'

As Jack said those words there was a *Knock*! *Knock*! *Knock*! at the door. Jill answered it and there stood the devil. He had not forgotten how Jack had tricked him in the past.

'Hello,' said the devil. 'I'm here to see the sick man.'

Jill gasped. 'You? You're not welcome here. Be gone!'

But Jack called out, 'No! Come in, come in! I'd give you anything to take away the pain. You can have my house, you can have my apple tree, take it all!'

'I don't want your house or your tree,' the devil hissed. 'I want your *soul*!'

'You can have it! You can have it! Just take way the pain!' screamed Jack.

The devil slammed his pitchfork into the ground and the pain instantly disappeared.

'I'll be back for you in seven years,' smiled the devil. 'Ta-ta!'

The devil then walked out of the house.

'Oh Jack,' sighed Jill. 'What have you done this time?'

But Jack gave her a mischievous wink and a smile.

Jack and Jill lived happily for seven years, but there eventually came a *Knock*! *Knock*! *Knock*! at the door. Jack answered it and there stood the devil.

'Are you ready to come with me?' asked the devil.

'I just need a moment to say goodbye to Jill,' said Jack glumly. 'Would you like to come in and have a seat by the fire?'

'Thank you, I will,' the devil said as he sat in Jack's armchair.

Jack put on his coat and said goodbye to Jill. He then turned to the devil and said: 'Come on, then.'

The devil tried to get up, but found that he was stuck in the chair.

'What's going on here?' bellowed the devil. 'Why can't I get out of this chair?'

The devil pulled and pushed, heaved and hauled, but no matter what he did, he just couldn't get out of that armchair.

'You'll not be able to get out unless I give you permission,' laughed Jack. 'And I'll not do that unless you give me another seven years.'

'*What*? boomed the devil. 'Not a chance!'

'All right, then. I'm off out – see you later!' said Jack.

'*No!*' the devil screeched. 'I don't want to sit here. What if the fire goes out? I'll be cold! All right Jack, you've got seven years, but then I'll be back!'

The devil was given permission to stand and then stormed out of the house in a terrible rage.

Jack and Jill lived happily for another seven years, but then there came another *Knock! Knock! Knock!* at the door.

Jack answered it and there stood the devil.

'Are you ready to come with me this time?' asked the devil angrily.

'Would you not like a sit down before we go?' Jack said.

'*No!*' thundered the devil.

'All right,' said Jack sadly. 'Let's go.'

Jack put on his coat, said goodbye to Jill and both he and the devil walked through his back garden.

Just then Jack said, 'Have you seen my apple tree? Isn't that the nicest apple tree you've ever seen?'

'Yes, it's very nice. I'm quite fond of apples myself,' said the devil.

'Would you just get me one apple for the journey, please?' asked Jack.

'Oh, all right,' said the devil as he reached over and grabbed an apple. But as he tried to pull it from the tree, he found that he was stuck to the apple.

'What's going on here?' demanded the devil. 'Why can't I let go of this apple?'

'You'll not be able to let go unless I give you permission,' laughed Jack again. 'And I'll not do that unless you give me another seven years.'

'*W– what?*' spluttered the devil. 'No way! Not this time!'

'All right, then. I'm going to the pub. I hear it's going to be a *cold* night! See you later!'

'*No!*' the devil screamed. 'I don't want to be stuck here! All right Jack. You've got another seven years, but then I'll be back!'

The devil then fumed out of the back gate in a terrible rage.

Jack and his wife lived happily for yet another seven years, but once again there was a *Knock! Knock! Knock!* at the door. Jack answered it and there stood the devil.

'No tricks,' said the devil. 'Let's go.'

Jack put on his coat and said goodbye to Jill. Then he and the devil walked through the back garden.

'Would you not like an apple for the journey?' asked Jack.

'I don't want any of your wretched fruit!' screamed the devil.

'Fair enough,' said Jack.

They walked along a muddy track in silence until Jack said, 'Oh! I know where we are! This is where I used to play as a child. We used to play jump in the sack.'

'Jump in the sack? What's that?' asked the devil.

'It's easy,' said Jack, pulling his sack from his coat pocket and placing it on the ground. 'You go into the sack and out of the sack, into the sack and out of the sack, into the sack and out of the sack, like that.'

The devil watched Jack jumping in and out of the sack and said, 'That's the stupidest game I've ever seen!'

'It's only because you can't do it!' challenged Jack.

'Nonsense,' scoffed the devil. 'Stand back and watch this!'

The devil leapt into the sack but found that he was stuck and couldn't get back out.

'What's going on here?' demanded the devil. 'Why can't I get out of this sack?'

'You'll not be able to get out unless I give you permission,' laughed Jack. 'And I'll not do that unless you give me another seven years.'

'Never!' screamed the devil. 'Not a chance! Not this time.'

'All right, then,' said Jack, and he pulled the sack up and over the devil's head, tied a knot and shouted, 'Who wants a game of footie?'

Everyone ran from their houses and into the street.

'Where's the ball?' someone asked.

'I haven't got one,' beamed Jack. 'We'll just have to use this sack.'

The football match went on for a full 90 minutes with 22 players kicking the sack up and down the street. At the end of the 90 minutes, no one had scored. So they played a further 30 minutes of extra time. Then there were penalties – five each.

'All right,' came a whimpering voice from the sack. 'You can have your seven years, just stop kicking me!'

Jack opened the sack and poured the devil on to the ground. The devil literally pulled himself together and staggered off.

Jack invited everyone back to his house for a party. There was drinking and dancing. Then, in the middle of it all, Jack had a heart attack and collapsed dead on the floor. His spirit went drifting up and up to heaven. At the pearly gates he met St Peter himself.

'Hello!' said Jack cheerfully. 'Can I come in, please?'

'I'm afraid not, Jack,' answered St Peter. 'You've been making deals with the devil. It's downstairs for you.'

So Jack's spirit went drifting down and down into hell. At the gates of hell, Jack knocked and waited.

A little demon opened a small hatch in the gate and screeched, 'What do you want?'

'Hello!' said Jack, less cheerfully. 'Can I come in, please?'

'Just a minute and I'll check!' the demon squeaked and went off to find the devil.

'It's Jack from Ireland,' the demon said, once he'd found the devil. 'Can he come in?'

'*No*!' boomed the devil. 'Tell him to go away!'

The demon went back and screeched, 'We don't want you – go away!' and slammed the hatch shut in the gate loudly. Jack's spirit went floating back up to Ireland where he drifted here and there, from place to place in the dark. St Peter saw Jack and, feeling sorry for him, came down from heaven and gave Jack a little light to guide his way. From that day on, Jack lit paths for travellers and helped people find their way home. Some people call this light 'will-o-the-wisp'. The next time you walk around late at night, keep looking for the light of 'Jack-o'-lantern'.

About this story

Jack-o'-lantern carving was invented in Ireland and is now practised all over the world. The lanterns are meant to scare away ghosts and spirits who prefer to hide in the darkness. The ghost in the beginning of this Jack story appeared scary at first, but then changed once Jack spoke kindly to it. We can use this part of the story to write some opposite descriptions of our own.

Teaching idea: Adjectives

Ask the children to write a list of adjectives to describe a scary ghost character such as grotesque, horrific, noxious, lethal, terrifying, sickening, gruesome, horrifying, bloodcurdling or sinister.

Then the children could create a list of antonyms for an opposite description such as friendly, gentle, calm, quiet, soothing, cheerful, relaxed, pleasant, bright or delightful.

The website wordhippo.com could also be used to find further adjectives by typing in 'scary' on the 'Synonyms' page, but also opposite adjectives on the 'Antonyms' page.

Once the children have both lists, they could begin to describe a scary ghostly figure that turns kindly or perhaps even the other way around. An example of this can be seen in the film *Percy Jackson and the Lightning Thief*. Percy's teacher turns into a Fury during a trip to the museum. The clip can be found on Youtube at: www.youtube.com/watch?v=fnAJy5ITWME and demonstrates a normal-looking character who turns into a scary one.

Perhaps the children could add some setting description that changes as the character changes, too. An example of this is whenever the Dementors arrive in the Harry Potter books. As soon as these characters appear, the setting becomes frozen and the air is filled with a chilling fog. The whole atmosphere and mood in J. K. Rowling's setting descriptions are altered by the presence of the Dementors.

The children could replicate this by describing the landscape that matches the mood of the ghostly character in it. A scary ghost might be haunting a cold, dark and bitter place, but when the ghost changes to become friendly, then the place becomes warmer, brighter and more pleasant.

20 Sir Gawain and the Green Knight (Welsh)

There are many stories of Sir Gawain. This story and the one of the 'Loathly Lady' are perhaps the most famous. The Arthurian legends are British and likely originate from Cornwall. The story here was written as a poem during the fourteenth century in England, but its origins are from the twelfth century in Wales. Gawain is mentioned under the name Gwalchmei in some of the earliest Welsh Arthurian sources. The Green Knight is named Bertilak in some versions and Bredbebble in others. In one version it is the sorceress and enemy of King Arthur, Morgan le Fay, who transforms a knight into a Green Man. In folklore across the UK, green is the colour of rebirth. It is in this story that the Knights of the Round Table, in particular Sir Gawain, are taught to be truthful and are therefore reborn as better people.

Sir Gawain and the Green Knight

It was Christmas Day in the court of Camelot. The Knights of the Round Table were all excitedly gathered around waiting to start their Christmas dinner, but no one would begin until King Arthur himself had arrived.

The whole castle was bustling with excitement as King Arthur and Lady Guinevere walked into the court.

'Merry Christmas to you all! We shall begin our feast shortly,' smiled King Arthur. 'But first, tell me something brave that you have done this year, my knights.'

Everyone looked at each other. Everyone looked at King Arthur. Everyone shrugged their shoulders.

'Really, you are too modest, my knights!' laughed the king. 'Tell me your brave acts!'

'Erm, I've been down into the dark cellar!' said one knight.

'I got a spider out of my room!' said another.

'I've been down the big slide!' another called.

'This is ridiculous!' boomed King Arthur. 'We are supposed to be the bravest knights in the world. Nobody can have their Christmas dinner until I hear of at least one act of bravery.'

A great groaning sound echoed throughout the court.

Suddenly, the door burst open and in walked a Green Knight. His armour was green, his boots were green and he led a green horse into the large room. The Green Knight then took off his green helmet showing his green face. His skin was green, his hair, his beard and even his teeth were green.

'I am the Green Knight from the Green Chapel!' he thundered. 'I have heard that the Knights of the Round Table are the bravest in the world! I am here to find out!'

'What is it you want?' asked King Arthur.

'To set a challenge!' answered the Green Knight. 'I ask if *anyone* here is brave enough to take my green axe and chop off my head! But you must then travel to my Green Chapel by next Christmas and *I* will get to do the same thing to *you*!'

Everyone gasped.

'Who will take up my challenge?' roared the Green Knight.

Everyone looked at each other. Everyone looked at the Green Knight. Everyone shrugged their shoulders.

Eventually, King Arthur stood up and declared, 'If none of my knights will do it, then I shall!'

Sir Gawain then leapt to his feet and shouted, 'No, my cousin. I will take up the challenge!'

The whole court burst into applause as Sir Gawain walked towards the Green Knight. Secretly, Sir Gawain was thinking that if *he* chopped off the Green Knight's head, then how could that knight chop off Sir Gawain's head next Christmas or any other Christmas? The Green Knight would be dead.

'You are truly brave, Sir Gawain,' smiled the Green Knight while kneeling down. 'Take my axe.'

Sir Gawain took the green axe and with one swing he chopped off the Green Knight's head. The head rolled to the other side of the court, then stopped and was staring at Sir Gawain. The green body was slumped on the floor. All was silent and still.

Then, the green body stood up! It walked over to the green head, picked it up and stuck it back onto the neck.

The Green Knight slowly turned to Sir Gawain.

'Well done!' he smiled with a green grin. 'Seven days before Christmas, seven green geese will fly above Camelot. Follow them. They will lead you to my Green Chapel.'

The Green Knight then led his green horse out of the door. Everybody burst into applause again.

'Well done, my cousin!' smiled King Arthur. 'You are truly the bravest of my knights. Now we can eat!'

All the knights began talking and eating at once. Only Sir Gawain sat in silence. He stared at his dinner with his mouth hanging open, not believing what had just happened.

Winter turned to spring. Then summer arrived. Autumn followed and then it was winter again. The seven green geese circled Camelot as Sir Gawain got his horse, Gringolet, ready. The whole of the court of Camelot waved and cheered as the knight rode on his way following the green geese.

On the first day of his journey, Sir Gawain met a dragon in the forest. He charged with his sword drawn and defeated the dragon in no time.

On the second day, he met a three-headed giant who tried to eat Gringolet. Sir Gawain chopped off the three heads in a flash.

On the third day, the green geese circled above a castle and then disappeared. So Sir Gawain knocked at the door and a rich lord answered.

'Hello!' smiled the lord. 'Welcome to my castle!'

'I am Sir Gawain from Camelot. I have been following seven green geese to find the Green Chapel. I must be there by Christmas Day. Do you know the way? The geese I was following seem to have disappeared.'

'Yes, of course. The Green Chapel is only a day from here. You are early, so why not rest here for three nights? You can eat and sleep as much as you want, then I will take you to the Green Chapel.'

Sir Gawain smiled and thanked the rich lord.

After dinner, Sir Gawain and the rich lord sat by the fire talking like old friends.

'Why don't you have a long rest in the morning?' smiled the rich lord. 'I'll go out hunting. Whatever I get tomorrow, I will give to you as a gift. But if you are given anything in my castle, then *you* must give it to *me*. How does that sound?'

Sir Gawain laughed and agreed.

The next morning, Sir Gawain woke late. The sun was shining through the windows and the rich lord had been hunting since daybreak. Sir Gawain suddenly noticed the lord's wife sitting on his bed staring at him.

'What are you doing in my bedroom?' he shrieked.

'I've come to give you a kiss!' she smiled.

'A kiss?' gasped Sir Gawain. 'Certainly not! Now leave my room so I can get dressed!'

But the lord's wife refused to go. She spent the whole day talking and laughing with Sir Gawain.

Eventually, the door of the castle opened and the rich lord could be heard calling for Sir Gawain.

'You must go or your husband will be angry!' said the knight.

The lord's wife then kissed Sir Gawain on the cheek and rushed out of his room. The knight got dressed and rushed to greet the lord.

'Sir Gawain!' smiled the rich lord. 'I have been hunting all day and have caught a deer which I give to you. Have you been given anything today?'

Sir Gawain shrugged his shoulders, walked over and kissed the lord on his cheek.

'Blurgh!' the lord stepped back rubbing his cheek. 'Is that all you were given? Never mind, let us eat dinner.'

After their meal, Sir Gawain and the lord sat by the fire again.

'Why don't you have another long rest in the morning?' smiled the rich lord. 'I'll go out hunting again and whatever I get I will give to you as another gift. But if you are given anything in my castle, then you must give it to me. Do you agree?'

Sir Gawain laughed and agreed for a second time. He woke up late and saw that the lord's wife was sitting on his bed for a second morning.

'What are you doing in here again?' he demanded.

'I've come to give you another kiss!' she smiled.

'Again?' gasped Sir Gawain.

The lord's wife spent another day talking and laughing with the knight. Like the day before, the door of the castle eventually opened and the rich lord could be heard calling for Sir Gawain.

'Go now or your husband will be angry!' he said.

The lord's wife then kissed Sir Gawain on the other cheek and rushed out of his room. The knight got dressed and rushed to greet the lord.

'Sir Gawain!' smiled the rich lord. 'I have been hunting all day again and have caught a wild boar which I give to you. Have you been given anything today?'

Sir Gawain shrugged his shoulders and walked over and kissed the lord on his other cheek.

'Blurgh!' the lord stepped back rubbing his cheek. 'Is that all you were given again? Never mind, let us eat dinner!'

After their meal, Sir Gawain and the lord sat by the fire and again made the same deal.

Sir Gawain awoke late and saw that the lord's wife was sitting on his bed for a third morning.

'Not again,' he mumbled. 'I suppose you're here to give me a kiss, then?'

'No,' she smiled. 'I have come to give you a different gift.'

She pulled out a green belt and held it out to Sir Gawain.

'This belt will protect you from any harm. No sword, arrow or axe will hurt you. Good luck with the Green Knight tomorrow.'

Sir Gawain put on the belt and got dressed.

'Sir Gawain!' smiled the rich lord when he returned from hunting. 'I have been hunting all day again and have caught a red fox which I give to you. Have you been given anything today?'

'No,' said Sir Gawain. 'Nothing.'

'Nothing?' asked the rich lord.

'No, nothing,' answered the knight while rubbing the green belt.

After their meal, the rich lord told Sir Gawain to meet him early and he would take him to the Green Chapel.

The next morning was Christmas morning. Sir Gawain and the rich lord set off early. They arrived at the Green Chapel in no time.

'This is where I must leave you, my friend,' said the rich lord as they stood on a green, grassy bank.

Sir Gawain gulped. The rich lord rode away on his horse and just then the Green Knight appeared.

Sir Gawain rubbed the green belt around his waist nervously.

'Are you ready?' thundered the Green Knight.

Sir Gawain nodded as he kneeled in front of the green man showing the back of his neck. The Green Knight slowly raised his green axe and brought it swinging down on to Sir Gawain's neck. But before it hit the neck, the Green Knight stopped.

Sir Gawain looked up. The Green Knight brought the axe swinging down again, but he stopped the axe from hitting this time, too. Sir Gawain shivered. The Green Knight then brought the axe swinging down a third time and this time he cut the back of Sir Gawain's neck. Warm blood trickled down.

'Get up,' smiled the Green Knight.

Sir Gawain slowly got up and in a flash of green light the Green Knight disappeared and there stood the *rich lord*.

'I am the Green Knight of the Green Chapel *and* I am the rich lord. I tested your honesty by asking you to give me what you had been given in my castle. What were you given by my wife yesterday?"

'I was given this green belt by your wife. I'm sorry I didn't tell you. I thought it would protect me. I should have kept my promise.'

'Keep the belt,' smiled the rich lord. 'It will not protect you from harm, but it will remind you to *always* tell the truth.'

Sir Gawain nodded. He understood the lesson that the Green Knight had taught him. He understood that the bravest thing of all is to tell the truth. He waved goodbye to the rich lord and rode Gringolet all the way back to Camelot. When he arrived, the knights were all gathered outside waiting nervously for him.

'Sir Gawain!' beamed King Arthur. 'You are all right – we were so worried!'

Sir Gawain told his story in the courtroom that night. It was decided from that day on that all the Knights of the Round Table should wear green belts to remind them all to always tell the truth. They did exactly that. Their truth made them the bravest knights that ever lived.

About this story

Morals feature in many Arthurian legends in which the knights have to follow a chivalrous code. The moral in this story is always to tell the truth.

Teaching idea: Morals

Ask the children to think of other things that we should always do and things that we should never do. You could suggest a few to get the discussion going such as:

Always

- be friendly;

- be kind to others;

- be respectful;

- follow school rules;

- try your best;

- recycle;

- look after the environment;

- try to be healthy;

- be active.

Never

- hurt anyone;

- say mean things;

- break things;

- drop litter;

- judge people;

- judge yourself;

- take life too seriously;

- be cruel to animals;

- dwell on mistakes for too long.

The children could discuss in small groups things they feel that they should always do and never do. Then they should choose one thing to plan a story around. To keep with the theme of the Sir Gawain story, they could begin with a knight character who makes the wrong choice. In the story, Sir Gawain chose to lie to the rich lord about the gift he was given. He chose not always to tell the truth. Using this as a model, a knight may drop litter everywhere they go or say mean things to the other knights of the castle.

Knights wore heraldic colours and each colour had a different meaning.

Red = strength

White = peace

Blue = loyalty

Yellow = generosity

Green = rebirth

Brown = victory

Purple = justice

Black = sadness

Pink = love

In the story above, the Green Knight teaches Sir Gawain to be reborn as a truth teller. The children could choose a colour for a new knight character who teaches their other character a lesson. A red knight might use his strength to clean up the environment after the other knight drops litter everywhere. The naughty knight might then see how much better the castle and land look once they are cleaned up and so change their ways.

A pink knight might pay compliments to all the other knights and his many friends. The knight who keeps saying mean things has no friends and is taught by the pink knight how to be kind to others, which leads to friendship.

The children could plan their own narrative using their two characters with the chosen colour and moral to be learnt.

Conclusion

Bruno Bettelheim explains how fairy tales, myths and legends educate, support and liberate the emotions of children in his book *The Uses of Enchantment*. These traditional tales are powerful developmental tools for children and adults alike. They can have a dark side to them, but generally good overcomes evil. They frequently contain moral messages, too, and are useful tools for promoting oral storytelling. They follow themes and structures still seen in modern writing – for example, *The Gruffalo* feels like a traditional tale as it has the rule of three, just like *Goldilocks*, *The Billy Goats Gruff* and countless others.

In Rick Riordan's books, he uses the Ancient Greek myths as a basis for his *Percy Jackson* books and Ancient Egyptian myths as inspiration for his *Kane Chronicles* books. In *Percy Jackson and the Lightning Thief*, the plot follows all the rules of the traditional tale, with its triadic structure and themes of good versus evil.

Modern books like these still follow the structure and themes of the traditional tale because they have an everlasting appeal. The themes can be dark, but children still adore them as they excite and inspire. They appeal to all ages essentially because human beings are story animals. We thrive on them in all of their forms, whether news articles, stories in the pub or experiences at work that we share at the dinner table. We communicate through story. We express our inner selves in the retelling of the story.

Stories hold great power. I hope that this book will give you great power in the classroom – the power to inspire writing!

Adam Bushnell

Bibliography

Ashe, R and Ashe, G (1973) *Folklore, Myths and Legends of Britain*. London: Reader's Digest.

Bettelheim, B (1999) *The Use of Enchantment: The Meaning and Importance of Fairy Tales*. London: Penguin.

Carroll, L (2013) *The Jabberwocky and Other Nonsense: Collected Poems*. London: Penguin Classics.

Davies, S (2008) *The Mabinogion*. Oxford: Oxford University Press.

Jacobs, J (1993) *English Fairy Tales*. London: Children's Classics.

Jacobs, J (2011) *Celtic Fairy Tales*. London: Pook Press.

Kidd, M (2020) *Scottish Fairy Tales, Myths and Legends*. London: Scholastic.

O'Donoghue, B (2006) *Sir Gawain and the Green Knight*. London: Penguin Classics.

Various authors (2020) *The Anthology of Irish Folk Tales*. Cheltenham: The History Press.

Westwood, J and Simpson, J (2005) *Lore of the Land: A Guide to England's Legends, from Spring-heeled Jack to the Witches of Warboys*. London: Penguin.

Index